NIGHT PLEASURES

Dave Smith was born in Portsmouth, Virginia, in 1942, educated at the University of Virginia, Southern Illinois University, and Ohio University. He has published a novel, *Onliness* (1981), a collection of short fiction, *Southern Delights* (1984), and a collection of essays on contemporary American poetry, *Local Assays* (1985). He is also editor of *The Pure Clear Word: Essays on the Poetry of James Wright* (1982) and co-editor (with David Bottoms) of *The Morrow Anthology of Younger American Poets* (1985). He is currently co-editor of *The Southern Review* and Professor of Twentieth Century Literature at Louisiana State University in Baton Rouge, Louisiana.

Night Pleasures: New & Selected Poems (Bloodaxe Books, 1992) is his first book of poems to be published in Britain, and brings together his latest work in the title collection at the end of the book, as well as poems from ten previous collections, including *The Roundhouse Voices* (Harper & Row, 1985) and *Cuba Night* (William Morrow, 1990).

NIGHT PLEASURES

NEW & SELECTED POEMS

Dave Smith

BLOODAXE BOOKS

ISBN: 1 85224 131 4

First published 1992 by
Bloodaxe Books Ltd,
P.O. Box 1SN,
Newcastle upon Tyne NE99 1SN.

Bloodaxe Books Ltd acknowledges
the financial assistance of Northern Arts.

Cover printing by J. Thomson Colour Printers Ltd, Glasgow.

Printed in Great Britain by
Cromwell Press Ltd, Broughton Gifford, Melksham, Wiltshire.

In memory of
Mary Alice Cornwell,
and
Ralph Gerald Smith

Contents

Acknowledgements

I wish to express gratitude for fellowships which have, over the years of the composition of these poems, been critically helpful to me. I am especially indebted to the National Endowment for the Arts for Fellowships in Poetry, to the John Simon Guggenheim Foundation, to the Lyndhurst Foundation of Chattanooga, Tennessee, and to the Virginia Arts Commission.

'The Fisherman's Whore', 'Near the Docks', 'Among the Oyster Boats at Plum Cove', 'The Shark in the Rafters', 'Rooster Smith's Last Log Canoe', 'The Spinning Wheel in the Attic', 'Hard Times, But Carrying On', 'Hammy's Boat Circling Through the Moon', 'The Powerless House', and 'Mending Crab Pots' are reprinted from *The Fisherman's Whore* by Dave Smith, copyright © 1974 by Dave Smith, reprinted by permission of the Ohio University Press.

'When the Fiddlers Gather', 'First Hunt at Smithfield', 'On a Field Trip at Fredericksburg', 'For the Polioed Girl Killed by Cottonmouths', 'How to Get to Green Springs', 'Cumberland Station', 'The Spring Poem', 'Picking Cherries', 'Boats', 'The Perspective & Limits of Snapshots', 'Hole, Where Once in Passion We Swam', 'Pink Slip at Tool & Dye', 'Night Fishing for Blues' are reprinted from *Cumberland Station* by Dave Smith. Copyright © 1971, 1973, 1974, 1975, 1976 by Dave Smith. Reprinted by permission of the University of Illinois Press and *The New Yorker*. Some of these poems originally appeared in *The New Yorker*.

'Goshawk, Antelope', 'Under the Scrub Oak, A Red Shoe', 'The White Holster', 'The Collector of the Sun', 'Hawktree', 'Black Widow', 'August, On the Rented Farm', 'Waving', 'A Moment of Small Pillagers', 'The Dark Eyes of Daughters', 'Pine Cones', 'Rain Forest', and 'In the Yard, Late Summer' are reprinted from *Goshawk, Antelope* by Dave Smith, copyright © 1979 by Dave Smith, reprinted by permission of the University of Illinois Press and *The New Yorker*. Some of these poems first appeared in *The New Yorker*.

'Halloween Delight', 'Bluejays', 'Desks', 'Pond', ' Homage to Edgar Allan Poe', 'Portrait of a Lady', 'Waking Under a Spruce with My Love', 'Elk Ghosts: A Birth Memory', 'Wedding Song', and 'Reading the Books Our Children Have Written' are reprinted from *Homage to Edgar Allan Poe* by Dave Smith, copyright © 1981 by Dave Smith. Published by the Louisiana State University Press. 'Portrait of a Lady' first appeared in *The New Yorker*.

'Elegy in an Abandoned Boatyard', 'The Tire Hangs in the Yard',

to reprint poems they first published: *College English* ('Elegy for Hollis Summers'), *The New Yorker* ('Basement Waltz', 'Wreckage at Lake Ponchartain', 'Night Pleasures'), *The Southern Review* ('The History of the Queen City Hotel', 'Lyons' Den'), *Verse* ('Graduation'), *The Virginia Quarterly Review* ('Pulling a Pig's Tail').

FROM **THE FISHERMAN'S WHORE**

(1974)

The Fisherman's Whore

Like gentle swells
of corn rows that will not fade
    from a golf course fairway,
        or old burial mounds,
    dead boats in low silhouettes

        rise from a hump,
from black marsh mud-beaded where
    the town's trash leaches in
        bright water-blisters.
Our fathers' worn whores wait.

    Along the swing burdened
porches of whitewashed houses you
    can hear the lacy swamp grass
        hiss underfoot, bladed
    now in winter's first wind.

    Rattling their throats
fishermen, old, come to sag once more
    against the one caved-in, gone
        gray as memory's lies
    they scatter to the tides.

    Mother-of-pearl garlands
their flanks. Scales, seaworm skins,
    shells flash sun like jewels
        from womanly curves no
    flush of blood freckles darker.

    Rust wells steadily out
of pine, yet tight are a few joints.
    Passion's hulks, ulcered, too
        weak to bear men safe,
    beaten by thudding seas, they

        hold our unforgotten ways.
Where else shall we find ourselves
    dreaming awake, cradled inside
        chines' thigh and bow,
    unbroken fables of the fathers?

Today another son goes,
bicycle stacked by a sewered creek,
   to chip, to paint, to sing
      in love's raw grip
   for whatever water offers him.

Near the Docks

There was a fire in the night.
Across the street I slept among the others
as the ashes snowed upon small pines.
I slept, and owned nothing, a child ignorant
of fortune's blistering story, the playful
flash in the dark, the unseen smolder
that would leave us revealed, though
unchanged as the black earth.
I said my prayers for luck
like the man trying to live
in two houses, hoping for time
to leave the old one of his fathers,
its windows with weariness fogged.
The other was half-built, roofless,
green timbers going gray in sun
like a vision that would not be done.

I had climbed there all summer to smoke
after the hours when I would find him
hunched on his wooden stool. Each
morning, halfway between the houses,
on his tongue would be the story
of how they came and of the sea,
his hands weaving wire to a trap,
making careful seams to catch
cunning scuttlers. I saw his wife
already had begun to hang her wash,
its shapes rueful, steaming, ghostly
in sunflare. That day a mongrel
lapped from the ruts of the fire trucks.

16

I thought little was changed by fire,
only his toolshed limp as a black sail
left in a heap, and that new hole
in the landscape. This was a poor place
where no one came, luckless, desperate,
eternal as guilt. I was the same
as the day before. In silence
I greeted that old one. Now I remember
seeing also, as if for the first time,
the shocking gray face of the sea
was his, fixed, in one quick glance.
It loomed up human and beautiful
as far off the figures of boats
crossed, worked, and seemed to sink
while they burned in the sullen sun.

Among Oyster Boats at Plum Cove

I have been away growing old
at the heart of another country
where there are no boats crumbling,
or small crabs with scuttling tools.
These pines warped with early snow,
this light that slopes and breaks
as the sea slides, sloughing
against your air, your earth-worn
flanks: I had loosed the dead
from memory but, coming back
confused, I find them waiting
here at the sea's rattling edge.

To them endlessly I bow, polite,
soiled, whiskered, wanting to drink,
to stand under the thick throats
with whiskey at Plum Cove, among
the booted ones with plaid shirts
and large loving hands. Full of tales
of kin and kind, I ask for words
hooked in their hold. When they groan,

or roll, villagers now sleeping off
wild hours among dwarf azaleas,
I taste rank air, a dead calm's turn.

The Shark in the Rafters

Under the stuttered snatch of the winch
they draw him by pulley and wheel,
the net-fouler unaccountably caught.
Slower than the night tracking
the sun through warm furrows
he rises into the open fishhouse
where sea's womb-blue lies
at a hole hacked in the house floor.

Not this mechanical screech but siren's
reedy crying blown out brings
the women from a darkness
of pine, through swamp grass
where age-ruptured boats hulk,
buried, decaying. Widows, wives,
they bluntly gaze like lovers
here at the land's last house,
no windows, no doors, just
the sun's tall fire, the wing
of shark swaying under the roof.

Beautiful, they watch the terrible
jaws jammed open again, the hook
spooning out the man's leg-stump,
blood-sluice flowing below them
into the minnow seeded water,
each surprised to feel risen
inside a finger's forbidden
touch: this hide is all
between them and sun's boil.
To open it at last, one
climbs with his knife, cheered
by the girls whose thighs burn

merely standing as one by one each
gore-tooth is made astonishingly
large, the great eye gouged,
tossed to small feeders, flesh
stripped out in tongues, a way
cut inside by bright coils
of bone, then there it is:
the heart, plain, dark
as a clock on a nightstand.
They cut it out, laughing,
and offer it up in parts
that fly like birds to hands.

Now the men grunt, hammerheaded,
as they pass dull meat to the women.
In an eyeblink gobbets, bloodied,
bob in ooze the tide draws
back to its salt slime, little
knots of flesh adrift in sun.
No one gives the shark a name
as they lug it home, hungry
at day's end, oddly buzzing
as if electrified by stars.

In rooms heavy with saltwater's
smell, daughters of daughters
stand close, whisper the tale:
an unwed woman is remembered.
A man moves over the sandy floor
to her bed, moon-shadow ticking,
dark deep around. The eyes grow
glazed, lips pull back, teeth
shine. They prepare the feast.
One peels the flesh, knife quick.
One fries, hands blistering.
Speaking of hurt, they begin
where the heart was beating
alone, the mouth hugely open.

Rooster Smith's Last Log Canoe

the Mariner's Museum, Newport News, Virginia

Suspended in a vast pendulum of blue light
they keep alive the legends of boats,
the whole evolution of their making

huddled beneath the giant bust
of an American Eagle
whose wings filter the sun, whose

talons press and hold a huge brass dial
which spreads time on the floor
like moss in a cove.

Each step drops a man deeper in the Eagle's
eye, and there is one room Rooster
lives in, a man recognizable

by the scars on his hand or the shy
shadowy way he poses by his last boat,
as if he is saying again and again

this one is for you, this I have well built.
His arm bends into the curved bow
and the chines of heartwood.

On the wall there is a series of photographs
as precise and stiff as half-inch
sheets of James River ice.

In the first, a tree, fully leafed, rippled
sunshine on the slack water in the rear.
Nothing else has happened.

Rooster stands then by the corpse of an ancient
trunk, his saw baring its teeth like a fish.
He seems sad or winded.

Two men, one shadowed and grim, one lighter, lean
into the hollowed body of wood, their faces
turned up, surprised. The river is flat.

A keel rises in the bladed reeds. Ribs glisten.
The men lean on each other; wood chips
fleck the gray earth like stars.

A mast leads the eye to the center of the river
where specks seem loose, errant, whipped
by winds. No men appear.

On Model-A wheels, she strains at the edge of
Deep Creek Point. Pines like massive wings
hover over the hull. Rooster looks

to the next photograph, where she is under way.
He is missing, and the other man.
It is marked THE LAST BAY CANOE.

Under the final frame, the green hull sleeps
in its chocks, a tree full of warm light,
its body groaning for water. Your hand,

which once swung from Rooster's calloused fingers,
presses the chines to feel where blade,
fire, sweat made their marks.

Some things do not show in two-dimensional gloss:
pain in the chest, arm-breaking knots.
Northeast storms escape this room.

But with the hand speaking to the wood, under
the Eagle's time-splintering gaze, a wind
in a wind begins to blow.

You listen the way a child does, feeling in
the open chinks and caulkless seams
for Rooster's empty bottles.

Everything is exactly as it was, the dark stain
on the stern seat, the heavy chain links
played out, the bird circling overhead.

In that dusk-deflected light you are told it keeps
your grandmother's torn skirt, a piece
the sea blew on in wood's belly.

The Spinning Wheel in the Attic

Not for beauty's sake, or art's, this wheel
    came round in his calloused palms,
        bent willows and oak,

formed for the work of spinning whole cloth,
    gatherer of scraps fine and coarse,
        a tool. Shuttle and stroke,

long nights he labored in the ways of stars.
    His back bowed with shafts of steel,
        hewing wheel and spoke

from the supple wood hardening him to a fist.
    No consideration of death's rot, no
        fear of time's warp

led him to lay on signature or sign. He finished
    undeceived by the things he made.
        He wore a plain brown hat.

I can see his whittle marks as faint as scars,
    and edges he'd fail to sand
        when he fretted at

the grain's refusal to have his slightest design.
    My finger drawn in years of dust
        shows the wood raw,

stained by sweat or blood, the secret knots
    clear now as wire buried in a limb
        that buckles the saw

into the flesh so the man must curse what he needs
    but bend in whatever weather to work,
        licking lips, clamping jaw,

while at the window the woman, stilled, watches him.
    Sometimes he imagines what she will
        weave, not the coverlet

she'll die under, cold on their bed, never that,
　　　that will rise from homespun thread
　　　　　from the crop he's planted

to feed the sheep he'll shear, the dirty skeins
　　　stinking on the floor. But the touch
　　　　　of beauty is her gift,

he thinks. She has no illusions. This is her work
　　　only: making a family cloth to keep
　　　　　off cold and harm. Wood

must serve, and serves to show glistening grooves
　　　where she drew together the threads,
　　　　　the seams, at times would

whimper in pain. But mostly sing. Think of him
　　　leaving this wheel in dark air, touching
　　　　　her cloth, the last good

shove returning it all in a single spooling instant,
　　　love's first star-groan, the plow-peeled
　　　　　tang of earth, her spine

sparking in hearthlight, spinning for babes and deaths,
　　　until it stood without use, a shadow he'd
　　　　　bang against, surprised

by his pain, then listening as it sang easily alone,
　　　beyond purpose or understanding, a voice
　　　　　out of the void, alive.

Hard Times, But Carrying On

His eyes were once blue and pure
     as the Bay, but that too
        turned thick with grim
trails of weeping oil and shapeless

hulls of paper whose words, bleached,
     seeped away on the slow flow.
        He owns the same boat, boots,
and seine he started with forty winters

back, when running in and out alone he'd
     boast, blind drunk: *on the nose!*
        He steers by a plain stick
and ropes, fancy wheels leave him cold.

He spits at big engines that stutter by
     in bad weather, confident
        of what's below, and knows
they ridicule the radar in his head,

the barometer in his bones, who shake
     the air with sleek wakes. He
        works his hole with craft,
eats fish for lunch at noon and dots

it with a lingering swallow of rye. Then
     drags back hard on the surging
        net, while all around the bags
crank up slack as widow's dugs in rain.

Hammy's Boat Circling through the Moon

This is the dream I have had
three nights in a row, the dream
of the eldest son sent to roar
over the Chesapeake Bay.

Hammy's skin is slippery.
It stinks and glitters.
He is drunk again.
He floats, he cannot swim.

The *Beulah*, her black nets
hung like a woman's veil,
wears forty-five skins of paint,
not one scraped or sanded.

Calm as breathing flesh, the Bay
might be the breast slipped loose
where Hammy's love lies down.
Moss drifts seaward, sleek as hair.

Then she's circling. Her piston,
tiny as a heart, pushes ripples
through ripples, rudder locked
like Hammy in bubbles and a wake.

I'll find him here, dog-paddling
drunk, calling his boat back,
barking at the moon's great hand
so full of him, but sliding off

as she rolls slowly around, goes
toward dawn, dog-nosed, to wait
alone where the moon does,
in the Bay's plate of hot stars.

The Powerless House

(in memory of Gilbert Page)

Out there in the marsh's soft middle, the dark
part cradles her house and I can find it
only by following the black wires that tremble
in the wind, powerless connections, dead

where something like a bomb, or someone's Ford,
out of control has ripped the night like
Vietnam, a sparkling wound that cuts all off
even to the last house where the young girl lies.

Her reddish hair cups her head like a pillow, she
is used to the gnats in it, and the heat.
She does not bother to bare her neck now, is
naked, and has been for a long time.

She holds her hand mirror and waits for lights
to come on, but her fingers see the hole
just between her ribs, and she believes everyone
lies to her. She dreams what could happen

when she rises, drifts up the long home-road,
looking for a guardpost in Asia, a bus stop
by the marsh in Virginia where they'll meet
when the power comes back. Gilbert,

why don't you tell her this dark is the dark
inside her old shoe, why the wind bores
through the side of her like a sniper's bullet,
why faces slide off her mirror in a house
where each switch is a nerve in a green body bag?

March Storm, Poquoson, Virginia, 1963

For three days the wind blew northeast,
reeds huddled underwater, bent back and down,
like birds with their heads bowed
in a winged darkness. The tide
held, came on slowly, not impelled
by high slopes to flood and churn
through narrows, but a lapping gray
light mounting the back steps: it came
unnoised, settled among our shoes
at the corners of closets, from
under sofas and rockers licked out
to sweep the rooms free of dust,
socks, dead mice, whatever would swim.

When the sun broke the fourth day's wake
the water retreated in silence,
the oyster boats sank, gentled
in the tops of the pines,
rudders lolling like dogs's tongues.
Stunned like drunks gone out
into abrupt noon light, we walked
through the fields, crowded
under the hulls' intimate shadows
to lift up our arms and show proof
of the scarred wounds seen at last
where we had always felt them.
All around us delicate seagrass
uprooted, rose and billowed until
each of us, lean as skeletal fish,
darted off as if to escape
the closing net of oncoming night.

Mending Crab Pots

The boy had run all the way home
from school to tell the old man
about a book he'd found which put
the whole thing in a new light:
'The beautiful sea, grandfather,
in a poem you might have written,
out there always to be touched
or swum in, or worked, or only
looked at, the way you told me.'

The old man gave the wire trap
one final twist, like a chicken's
neck, relit his dead cigar, said
he heard the slovenly bitch still
ranted around, couldn't be got
rid of, or lived with. He slit
the head from a blowfish, stuffed
it in the mouth of the pot, grinned.
'Them poets, goddamn'em, always
in school with their white hands.'

FROM **CUMBERLAND STATION**
(1977)

When the Fiddlers Gather

Now they are become more than men we must know how
                    to tune up, to take
        their flying root-and-stem light of joy
    from each old hand as it pumps under the dunesigh
        and wind blistered leaf, to learn
hunched on a rail merely to sing of water, of gulls,
                    of dusk shadowed like hope.

Each one, his time come, nods, clamps his jawbone in
                    patience like a crab's,
        years of notes loosed, spilling out, his
    silver hair drifting like shoreweed: he sways,
            pours himself forth, the sweat
on the wood dark as blood. Then another is rising to
            lift fiddle, to catch up

and counterstroke a strain, dying-out, that his gone
                    grandfather sang into
        the end like a man fearing God (so cries
    an untucking brother on his right). Buckling
            the song onward the next bows
with his boots tapping time against the dark frame of
            the bone fence. It must be

like entering a world where each breath has the dead
                    recklessness of tidal
        surge, song tuned on wave-fretted sealight,
    all the hardheaded laid-down fathers now slowly
            buoyed up as if in the world's
first Spring day, voices lapping in communion come
            simple as the lightning

to make hope cry for nameless, hardly to be believed
                    angels like these. Unseen
        they draw us by hedgerow and creek where
    the bow's graze grips, glides, the struck strings
            of lutes cry, making the poem
of the sailor's homesighting daybreak whistle, its
            prayer of welcome all ours.

First Hunt at Smithfield

Pulling in we're careful to be quiet, don't shut
doors, ease everything, careful as we cock
the Winchesters. No good, the farmer's bitch licks
a chain of barks, dirty chickens sound the alert.

                        You smoke. He's
up anyway because it's never early for a man
whose skin wakes without the lie of clocks.

A black snake slithers off the road we take,
his muscles ticking dew.
                   To me, to you, is it the same
high green, boil of yellows, black trunks of oak?
Where our road ends you angle off, camouflaged
almost, and almost hang like an aging leaf
under the eddying light, a shadow on that slope.
I hardly hear you whisper *here* but feel
my buttocks take the rotting trunk. What words
I have to bite back, thousands it seems.

You sweep the air like a hawk and load.

I know you'll calculate my shots, my time, break
your father's double, portion out the shells. Will I
do it right? So many things to think about,
each one my need to please you.
                     I watched the gray
creep in a fickle drift at your temple. I made
my eyes track the trees like yours. I learned
each knob, each distant sound, the way morning heat
tricked the wet leaves to sing with snapping, how
one shape implies a family, a line in wait.

               It was a long road back.
You dumped their bodies in a pile. Cold water
washed the tufts of fur from my small knife. Later
you tendered the farmer meat and smoked awhile
on the step of his truck. What you said was gone
before I heard it. I watched for that deep act
to pass between us, not knowing what it was. Dreaming

the dingy sinews of all those guts, the nights
and days we ranked ourselves together, I always
scrubbed the guns when we got home, made coffee
below the stairs, until your chair
stopped rocking, and your snore.

On a Field Trip at Fredericksburg

The big steel tourist shield says maybe
fifteen thousand got it here. No word
of either Whitman or one uncle
I barely remember in the smoke
that filled his tiny mountain house.

If each finger were a thousand of them
I could clap my hands and be dead
up to my wrists. It was quick
though not so fast as we can do it
now, one bomb, atomic or worse,
the tiny pod slung on wingtip,
high up, an egg cradled
by some rapacious mockingbird.

Hiroshima canned nine times their number
in a flash. Few had the time
to moan or feel the feeling
ooze back in the groin.

In a ditch I stand
above Mayre's Heights, the bookish
faces of Brady's fifteen-year-old
drummers, before battle, rigid
as August's dandelions
all the way to the Potomac
rolling in my skull.

If Audubon came here, the names
of birds would gush, the marvel
single feathers make
evoke a cloud, a nation,
a gray blur preserved
on a blue horizon, but

there is only a wandering child,
one dark stalk snapped off
in her hand. Hopeless teacher,
I take it, try to help her
hold its obscure syllables
one instant in her mouth,
like a drift of wind
at the forehead, the front door,
the black, numb fingernails.

For the Polioed Girl Killed by Cottonmouths
May 1960, Virginia Beach

On her birthday in the green-glowing season each year
    I hobble in my head to the ocean-side carnival
        where she screams. There the thrashing
           of winter's indifferent surf,

        closes my eyes so one stunned,
      soft face stands up in my own, comes
    alive, a distant candle's fuse, incandescent,
to glow with a beauty nothing can diminish or snuff.

I stand ghostly near parents I never have seen, knowing
    they placed her on that third birthday inside
        the heart of a musical, metal stallion,
           bound and strapped as she was

        so she might not fly wildly
      loose in fresh weather. I see them nod
    to one who holds a lever, who sets great gears
in motion as if he were God almighty, the world starts

to widen her eyes as it turns, a ponderous, creaky sail
        of iron painted like a meadow. From green, hurt
            hooks deep in her. I feel my own skull
                fall inward like sand, a flood

            against the nerves, a backsurge
        of ocean in the veins, hers, mine, but
    at fake dunewalls, drowning her while a woman's
voice whispers, too loud, *It's fear, it's only her fear.*

Around and around she rides, posing for the bulb's flash,
        no leverage in those legs enough to push off or
            unsay the deceit of words she has not
                learned to fear: *She'll live*

            all summer on this. On her body's
        flying joy, we mean, on delight's hot
    blood-shape of fish, duck, or a plunging horse.
This was her gift, after church one unseasonable Sunday

when the world was full of love. Even in her prayers
        what could be better for a girl than a canter?
            Oh joy and fear mixed in that heart!
                Each year despair bites me to

            feel Nature's needling teeth
        strike up and down those useless legs,
    as if it hates the shackles she wears to stand
every chance she gets. Even her flesh cannot say how it

needs help to do more than rise on those bones. Yet she
        screams as if she has seen the thousands they
            are, snakes no winter has prayed into
                church. Hateful hurt. If I

            call this Spring's accident,
        a sad, blind misunderstanding, a girl
    trapped by love blindly circling like a horse
by the sea, what has doomed her, whose bindings break not

though seawind yanks her hair and pain wells in a squeeze
        her father's hard arms wouldn't bring? What is so
            hideous it hides in each snapshot they
                keep striking on her birthday?

            Tonight, not remembering her
            day, only her fear as she spun loose
    from what spread inside, a small one's scream
comes out of the dark, like the soul terrified to death

as it whirls into vision. Whoever she was, as stranger I
        throb with that hurt. I shake my fist at the air
            at ourselves who are doomed, who
                save nothing but memory's cry.

How to Get to Green Springs

Nobody knows exactly when it fell off the map
or what the pressures were on its flooding river.
The hedge, the tottering mailbox – gone. That dimple
of light from the bicycle that raised itself to creak
at noon across a clattering bridge names my father.
His blood silent as a surging wish drags this town
lost through my body, a place I can get back to only
by hunch and a train whistle that was right on time.

But time and trains were never right in Green Springs,
West Virginia. What color could map the coal's grime,
shacks shored against the river every March, mail
left to rot because no one answered to occupant?
Farmers low on sugar cursed the heat and left cigars
boys would puff back to clouds where they dreamed
of girls naked as their hands under outfield flies.
Scores were low. There were no springs for the sick.
Women lined their walls with the Sears catalog, but
the only fur they ever had was a warbled rabbit.
To get here think of dirt, think of night leaking,
the tick of waterbugs, a train held in Pittsburgh.

Cumberland Station

Gray brick, ash, hand-bent railings, steps so big
it takes hours to mount them, polished oak
pews holding slim hafts of sun, and one
splash of the *Pittsburgh Post-Gazette.* The man
who left Cumberland gone, come back, no job
anywhere. I come here alone, shaken
the way I came years ago to ride down
mountains in Big Daddy's cab. He was
the first set cold in the black meadow.

Six rows of track, photographed, gleam, rippling
like water on walls where famous engineers steam, half
submerged in frothing crowds with something
to celebrate and plenty to eat. One engineer
takes children for a free ride, a frolic
like an earthquake. Ash cakes their hair.
I am one of those who walked uphill
through flowers of soot to zing
scared to death into the world.

Now whole families afoot cruise South Cumberland
for something to do, no jobs, no money for bars,
the old stories cracked like wallets.

This time there's no fun in coming back. The second
death. My roundhouse uncle coughed his youth
into a gutter. His son slid on the ice,
losing his need to drink himself
stupidly dead. In this vaulted hall
I think of all the dirt poured down
from shovels and trains and empty pockets.
I stare into the huge malignant headlamps
circling the gray walls and catch a stuttered
glimpse of faces stunned like deer on a track.

Churning through the inner space of this godforsaken
wayside, I feel the ground try to upchuck and I dig
my fingers in my temples to bury a child
diced on a cowcatcher, a woman smelling

alkaline from washing out the soot.
Where I stood in that hopeless, hateful room
will not leave me. The scarf of smoke I saw
over a man's shoulder runs through me
like the sored Potomac River.

Grandfather, you ask why I don't visit you
now you have escaped the ticket-seller's cage
to fumble hooks and clean the Shakespeare reels.
What could we catch? I've been sitting in the pews
thinking about us a long time, long enough to see
a man can't live in jobless, friendless Cumberland
anymore. The soot owns even the fish.

I keep promising I'll come back, we'll get out,
you and me, like brothers, and I mean it.
A while ago a man with the look of a demented cousin
shuffled across this skittery floor and snatched up
the *Post-Gazette* and stuffed it in his coat
and nobody gave a damn because nobody cares
who comes or goes here or even who steals
what nobody wants: old news, photographs
of dead diesels behind chipped glass.

I'm the man who stole it and I wish you were here
to beat the hell out of me because what you said
a long time ago welts my face and won't go away.
I admit it isn't mine, even if it's nobody's.
Anyway, that's all I catch today – bad news.
I can't catch my nephew's life, my uncle's,
Big Daddy's, yours, or the ash-haired kids'
who fell down to sleep here after the war.

Outside new families pick their way along tracks
you and I have walked home on many nights.
Every face on the walls goes on smiling,
and, Grandfather, I wish I had the guts
to tell you this is a place I hope
I never have to go through again.

The Spring Poem

Everyone should write a Spring poem.
LOUISE GLÜCK

Yes, but we must be sure of verities
such as proper heat and adequate form.
That's what poets are for, is my theory.
This then is a Spring poem. A car warms
its rusting hulk in a meadow; weeds slog
up its flanks in martial weather. April
or late March is our month. There is a fog
of spunky mildew and sweaty tufts spill
from the damp rump of a back seat. A spring
thrusts one gleaming tip out, a brilliant tooth
uncoiling from Winter's tension, a ring
of insects alongside, working out the Truth.
Each year this car, melting around that spring,
hears nails trench from boards and every squeak sing.

Picking Cherries

The ladder quakes and sways under me, old wood
I put too much faith in, like ancestors in hoods.
You circle me, cradling our baby, sun guttering
in your face, parading through leaves that hiss.
If I looked down I would know my fear calmed, see
in your narrowed eyes my body's ascent, deathless.
The bucket hangs from my belt, pulling obscenely
at my pants, but the cherries drop in and grow
one by one. I keep reaching higher toward the sun,
because I want those tartest on our tongues.
When I come down we will both be older, slowed,
but what of that? What is love but such climbing?
If the ladder gives way I still believe I can
catch one branch, drop the bucket and ease down.

Boats

1. *On the Poquoson River*

Rounding a slip of the marsh, the boat skids
under me and the propeller whines naked, digs,
then shoots me forward. A clapper rail
disappears in reeds and one white crane,
shaken from his nap, blinks and holds.

He makes me think of the Lost Tribe of Virginia,
as if the screech of insects was the Jew's
harp in John Jacob Niles's mouth. Redwings cry,
hidden like women mending nets too fine to see.

A creek opens its throat and I enter, dragging
down to hear the wake's slip-slop behind me,
thinking of the man who warned me people
were the same everywhere, lost and wondering

how they came to the life no one else wanted.
Sweet Jesus, he was right. Now he lies
in this sodden ground for the first time
in his life and I do not know even where.

Today is no different, the waters flood hulks
of empty houses, leaving beer cans to gleam
under the grinding moon. The first stalks
of narcissus break the ground with gold
though March still means tonight to freeze.

I know this place, its small mustering of facts
wind-worn and useless, real and repeated, the same
anywhere. At the end the creek leads to a room,
one placid boat swinging at a stick, pines sieving

air, the cleat ringing like small jewelry.

2. *The Cunner in the Calotype*

You need to know these boats, cunners, square
of bow and stern, never painted, always with a bottle
floating where the bilge is always rank and deep.
Sometimes they hold the sun like a butter tub but
nobody ever stepped a sail in one. They're used
to ferry out to where oyster scows squat, sere
and long as a lovely woman's thigh in a man's dream.
You need to ask why they lie cracked, sucking salt
water through the reed tubes, what has happened
to shove them back into the center of the marsh
where the screech of gnats goes out when a fisherman,
desperate in the end, shoves his finger in his ear.
You need to hear the slow toll of rope-ends, mossed
like drifting arms, the bell-cry of cleat and chained
transom stained a hundred hues by years of seas.

When bulldozers come to take the marsh, slapping down
layers of asphalt, when the all-temperature malls rise,
when women of the garden club cease their designing,
cunners will be gone, claimed by antique freaks, smashed
for scrap, the creeks leveled, the sun deceived with
only absence flashing in the heat. Once unemployed,
no swimming boys will sink them for a joke, no wind
whip and toss them in a storm or leave them in a tree.
Must fishermen exchange their daily lacks for jobs
behind counters? What rower of boats loves dirt?
What you get for one wouldn't pay for a week's beer.
But for them, fathers you need to know, I give you
this cunner of my place, its hand-hacked bottom whole
yet, the smell of crabs rank all over, a man's hat
floating in the black water as if mislaid, going down.

The Perspective & Limits of Snapshots

Aubrey Bodine's crosswater shot of Menchville,
Virginia: a little drama composing a little water,
specifically, the Deep Creek flank of the James.
Two-man oyster scows lie shoulder to shoulder,
as if you walk them, one land to another,
no narrow channel hidden in the glossy middle
like a blurred stroke, current grinning at hulls.
It is an entirely eloquent peace, with lolling
ropes and liquid glitter, this vision of traffic
and no oystermen in sight. Clearly Bodine is
not Matthew Brady catching the gropes frozen
at Fredericksburg with a small black box. So
well has he balanced the Mennonite church, yachts,
and country club, dignity's spare smell seeps.
His wide-angle lens foregrounds the bent teeth
of oyster tongs. Perhaps no Sunday bells toll.

Above the last boat, the flat-faced store squats
at the end of the dirt road as if musing over
accounts receivable. No doubt it has weathered
years of blood spilling. A spotted hound lifts
his nose above what must be yesterday's trash,
his white coat luminous at deep foliage. What
Bodine fails to show is the dog turning to lope
uphill under that screen of poplars, behind fat
azaleas that hide the county jail and drunks
starting to smell water's way out. Thumping
his noisy wife out a window, an oysterman cries
she cut him more than twice, madly mourning
their boy drowned twenty years. If he knew
Bodine had stood to snap the spot the boy died,
if we said a camera's yawn could suck back years
of his worst sailing shame, he would turn away.
He would whistle up mates in dignity's dust
and he would spit in his fists and would tell
his nameless black cellmate there are many men
for whom the world is neither oyster nor pearl.

Hole, Where Once in Passion We Swam

The sun frets, a fat wafer falling into a mouth of green.
I watch the pin-black of a mockingbird's eye cut sharply,
descend on the water, then emerge sleek, naked
as a girl who shimmered here, once, for me.

If we come back, penitents, to kneel at water, bass
scattering mayflies that often, in silence, graze lips,
what word floats out of the mouth unbearable, tiny
as a bird's grin? Not we, *me*. Giving it again I am

willing to believe whatever lives in mist sizzling stones.
I lift my head for echoes from trees, for flashed recoil
of flesh gaudy and wingless above the fists of the water
that crunched her like a beer can. Frogs honk

the only answer. Among them, a boy, I felt
the grotesque moon pull all night, peeled, went slowly
down in terror, rising, falling through the pulpy leaves
until the sun caught me, and I was no one wanted.

I walked away from knowing, to town, drank, calmly,
whatever I could, then slept. The hooks, in hairy hands,
clawed all smooth, searching in a fire of floodlights.
What could they find? I've been out of town a long time.

I wish the face floating above the chill at my knees
opened the door of a drab hotel. I wish it said
Go to hell or *Do you know what time it is?*, anything
that, if I heard, I could kneel to and swear to be faithful.

Pink Slip at Tool & Dye

He can only drink tea now, screwed and filed.
She is dead, in metal flecks.

55 years old and look like a bad nail
by God they yanked me out
I can tell you

soon as the hurt come son shut up
it don't mean nothing.

but listen: you got time for a ride?

Habit's put the glass in his hands, the brown
tasteless tea, slime, and cigarettes.
Every Sunday the same, old dog
fat at his feet.

Ain't so much me I'm asking for
dog like to get out and piss
think they remember.

Near the main gate of the Steel place I stop.
The amber light pours out of stacked horizons,
monstrous cranes hang over suburbs.

She think that piss mean something
it don't mean nothing.

Turning back in the dark, headlights flash
on our faces, bent, light of a woman's hair.

Night Fishing for Blues

At Fortress Monroe, Virginia,
the big-jawed Bluefish, ravenous, sleek muscle slamming
at rock, at pier legs, drives into Chesapeake shallows,
convoys rank after rank, wheeling through
flume and flute of blood, something
like hunger's throb hooking
until you hear it and know them there,
the family.

       Tonight, not far from where Jefferson Davis
hunched in a harrowing cell, gray eyes quick
as crabs's nubs, I come back over planks
deep drummed under boots years ago, tufts of hair

floating at my eyes, thinking it is right
       to pitch through tideturn and mudslur
       for fish with teeth like snapped sabers.
       In blue crescents of base lights, I cast hooks

baited with Smithfield ham: they reel, zing,
plummet, coil in corrosive swirls, bump on
scum-skinned rocks. No skin divers prowl here,

       visibility an arm's length, my visions

hand-to-hand in the line's warp. A meat-baited
lure limps through limbs nippling the muck,
silhouettes, shoots forward, catches a cruising Blue

       sentry's eye, snags, and sets

case-hardened barbs. Suddenly, I am not alone:
       three blacks plump down in lawn chairs, shudder,
       cast quick into the dark pod slopping under us. One

       ripples with age, a grandmotherly obelisk,

her breath puffing like a coal stove. She swivels
heavily, chewing her dark nut, humming gospel,
then spits thick juice like a careful chum.

       When I yank the first Blue
she mumbles, her eyes roll far out
a blue billowing of the sea. I hear her cant

to Africa, a cluck in her throat, a chain

song from the fisherman's house. I cannot
understand her yet. Bluefish pour at me in squads.
I haul two, three at a time, torpedoes, moon-shiners,
jamming my feet into the splintered floor, battling
whatever comes. Fathers, we have waited
a whole life for this minute. Dreams

graven on cold cell walls, Blues walk over

our heads, ground on back-wings, grind their teeth.
They splash rings of blue and silver around us, chevrons
of lost battalions. I can smell the salt of many ocean
runners, and now she hollers *I ain't doing so bad
for an old queen.* No time to answer. Two

car-hoods down her descendants swing

moonsleek arms, exotic butterflies: I hear them
pop beer cans, the whoosh released like stale breath
through a noose no one remembers. We hang

fast flat casts, artless, no teasing fishers,

beyond the book-bred lures, the pristine streams,
speeded-up, hungry, almost machines wound
too far, belts slipped, gears gone, momentum

hauling us to race at each other, winging

wildly as howitzers. Incredibly it happens: I feel
the hook hammer and shake and throw my entire weight
to dragging, as if I have caught the goddamndest

Blue in the Atlantic. She screams: *Oh my God!*

Four of us fumbling in beamed headlight and blue
arcs overhead cut the hook from her face. Gnats
nag us: I put it in deep and it must be gouged out
like old hate. When it is free, I hear Blues

not dead flop softly. I whisper it's luck
she could see us. She mops blood blued over
gold-lined teeth and opens her arms so her dress

billows like a caftan. She wants

nothing but to fish. I hand her a pole, then cast
as far as I can. She pumps, wings a sinker and hooks
into flashing slop and reels hard. In one instant both

      our lines leap rigid as daguerreotypes. We

have caught each other but keep on, pushed by blue
ghosts that thrash in the brain's deep cull.
We reel shadows until we see there is nothing,
then sit on the shaky pier like prisoners. Coil
by coil we trace the path of Bluefish-knots backward,

      unlooping, feeling for holes, testing,

slapping gnats like small fears. Harried, unbound,
at last we leap to fish again. But now a gray glow
shreds with the cloud curtain, an old belly-fire

      guts the night. Already the tide humps
on itself. Lights flicker like campfires in duty windows
at Ft. Monroe. She hooks up, saying *Sons they done
let us go.* I cast once more but nothing bites.

      Everywhere the circle of Blues stiffens

in flecks of blood. We kneel, stuff styrofoam
boxes with blankets of ice, break their backs
to keep them cold and sweet, the woman
showing us what to do. By dawn the stink has passed

      out of our noses. We drink beer like family.

All the way home thousands of Blues fall from my head,
falling with the gray Atlantic, and a pale veiny light
fills the road with sea-shadows that drift in figure

      eights, knot and snarl and draw me forward.

FROM **GOSHAWK, ANTELOPE**
(1979)

Goshawk, Antelope

Against snowpeaks, that country of blue sedge and shimmer
of distance rising into his tiny skull full of desire, he
fell across my windshield, a dot at sixty, and I, half

looking for a place I had never seen, half dreaming rooms
where blind miles of light lie on framed family faces,

saw him before he was anything, a spot above the glassy road
and in my eye, acetylene burned by brightness and hours
of passage. I saw memory. He came

out of the clouded horizon like the hummed dark of whipped
phone wires and the quiet of first feathering shingles
in storm or in the hour of burial,

and dropped into absence where the antelope stood alive
at the fence of barbed wire, horns lifted slightly,
hovering on hooves' edge as if bored with the prospect
of leaps, long standing and still. The wind

darted dust gave no image beyond itself, puffballs turned
clockwise and counter-clockwise as he stood
changeless beneath that sudden whistle
of gray. I felt my heart

within those lovely shoulders flame and try to buck off
what the air had sent down as shapeless as obsession
and stopped my car, knowing already how
easily the talons dispossessed

all who, without illusions, lived. Dark and light bucked,
clung, shredded in me until I was again a boy on a fence,
hunched near the dream-contending world. But

someone far off was calling and I could not undream
what held me. Though I stood at last it was late,
too late. Someone called. The legs I had always
trusted broke and I fell from all chance
to change what was done or undone.

In Wyoming, in June, it was already starcold
and the mild blue of dusk beat back my mother's pain
when I saw him, small as a wind, shriek for the cliffs,
his dream gone, the aching wingless antelope risen
from a low mound of rocks, running from what was
unseen and there, like the red print of a hand

about to fall, for I was late, wishing to God for a tree
to hide under and see for once what had died
out of my life but would never leave
or come back as it had been –
like the slow growth of
an antelope's legs into freedom
from a black whirling dream. It was late,
there had been no sign, no reason to move

except the call that might have been only dreamed, but
once I stood under the keening moon that, in Wyoming,
owns all that is and I begged the stars not to come
gouging my bitter and motherless sleep

where I lay long and longed, as I do now over barbed wire,
for the peace of the night-gleaming peaks, the flare
of absence that came, falling into

the accusing goshawk face of my father in that dark room
where I walked too late, where the glowing fur-tufts
of candle shadows drift on her face and his

and what was held has become, suddenly, lost like breath.

Under the Scrub Oak, A Red Shoe

Wrapped in twisted brown stockings, rolled, strangled
in our grandmothers's nylon, it was wedged at the heart
of what little cool shade ever accumulated there.
You would have to walk out of your way, back
along an arroyo twisting, empty as first memory,
back from the road out of town so far the sky
signals another world. To find it you do that,

though, in any case, you are simply walking: it appears,
something red shining through the gray-green glaze
of stunted limbs. If you were looking for a lost
child, steps deliberate and slow, you might see it.
Otherwise you will go on. Tonight it shines out,
having waited long to reveal itself, like an eye
in the darkness, and I innocently look into

its moment, imagining why it lacks a slender heel which
must, once, have nailed many boys against a wall
where she walked. I kneel and pick it up
as you would, hearing where she was
the moony insects cry around her, hearing also
the nylon like another skin scrape against my skin,

feeling the sound of its offslipping from her shaven calf,
a sound like the full-bellied hawk's when he floats.
In the arroyo no one could have seen her stop,
not as drunk as she pretended, sitting long
and, in time, methodically undressing, beyond
thinking now, placing her bundled shoe with care.
She must have been small. She would bear the usual

bruises, we would have had no fear of any we might add,
when we stood smoking by the wall, catcalling lightly.
It would have been one of those nights the breath
aches to be free of itself, of the body, then
she appeared in that red like first cactus buds,
something clearly wrong with her but that, by God,
no concern of any red-blooded boy she might want.
In the junked car someone squealed, someone
rose and fell. There were no names. I did not mean

whatever I said, but said it because she was so small.
She lay inside her fear, she shivered on her back.
Such moments we tell ourselves to walk away from,
and we do, as now I have walked in my hoping

for absence, but there is no absence, just
what waits, like a shoe, to reach, to say please
as best it can to whoever comes along, as if it
meant forgiveness, and love, as if any weather
that red skin endured was only the bruise
you might have kissed and might not yet refuse.

The White Holster

Ribbed, red glitter, those glass studs catch
and hold Christmas lights my mother raised.
Her hands cradle my one gift and behind
her black suit the little cedar
hides in blinking bulbs. Out
of light, at the elbow of stairs,
I wait to enter the room, still
a child, but already I know
the meaning of snow at windows,
like sand whipped and piled
until no place or time exists,
only the moment glassy as Jesus
hung in a matchbox. Ribbons
of newspaper drape the names
of our dead on needles. My feet
slide cold wood, feeling the way
down where she is in the middle
of the room where Christmas is always.

Long ago she called but I dawdled
in bed watching my thin breath,
wanting, not wanting to know

how poor we were, the war on,
our father gone. By each step
I grew larger and closer
to that waiting, and am
still only him with no gift
except words that bristle
like the bush she hacked out
of ice that night. I give
them back now, remembering
how long it takes to come to this

room where love stands for me – her face
bent over the white holster. The gun
silvers like flashed tracers or
snow across her breast and I
see it, my gift, leather,
stiff, white, with red tears
of glass, tufts of black fur
like wounds, the wild horse
ready to take me from darkness.
Her arms extend from the cedar's
frozen spine, her dress blinks
until I hear words, the room's
crisp needles rush and she
sweeps me to her, the diamond
glint of joy as her hand falls
on my hair still mine – *It is
what you wanted isn't it? His
last letter said you would want it.*

Tonight stars, in snowless December,
burst in endless explosions above
the cedar-skirted land until
there is no square inch
not gleaming and blinking.
At stair top, my hand flat
on the wall, switch off
so our tree squats alone,
I remember light iced
the floor where she was,
her black suit, my gift.

I thought: *I am happy*.
All day I would draw guns,
fighting like my fathers,
shaking the cedar like a bomb.
Happy, I shot at her, *happy*,
until at last the words
banged from her mouth as
she held me, saying *yes, yes*.

The Collector of the Sun

Through the small door of a hut
he stares at us, our movements,
the thousands of faces we are,
the booming world's roar

that, later, for a drifting instant,
he will enter. His extra shirt
tied by its arms for a sack,
he will be lost in his luck.

By the freeway, whipped as a weed,
he stalks the malignant ground
for bottles, and we wear on.
He doesn't imagine anyone

weeping in anger as he looms up.
And when he comes to the truck
parked, the woman asleep inside,
he thinks of his nights, wide

as the blue glare on the concrete,
full of glass and the clink-clink
of his business. For him sunset
is the good hour, the shapeless

beams of headlights always thick,
blending with sun to flick
off what he hunts. He is alone,
himself, dreaming of the blown

treasures of the world, the bottles
like loaves of gold. The rubble
of everything falls about him
like snow. He bends, reaches, grins,

and ignores whatever we scream.
His tarpaper walls are the dream
he has given himself. At night
a wind plays over the pipes

he has fashioned from glassy mouths.
The world seems right, as he lies out
in bed, but fingers itch, and a face,
oh, whose is it, leans like grace

and he can't remember whose or why.
At dawn, aching, he watches the sky,
sees dark birds pass, then us,
and is himself again, staring, blessed.

Hawktree

Tonight in the hills there was a light
that leaped out of the head
and yellow longing of a young boy.
It was Spring and he had walked
through the toy-littered yards
to the edge of town, and beyond.
In the tall spare shadow of a pine
he saw her standing, her skin
whiter than the one cloud
each day loaned to the long sky,
whiter even than the moon.

But she would not speak to one
who kept her name to himself
when boys laughed in the courtyard.
He watched her burn like a candle
in the cathedral of the needles.
After a while he saw the other light,
the sun's leveling blister, bring
its change to her wheaten hair.
In growing dark he waited, certain
she would hear the pine's whisper,
counting on Nature's mediation.
But she would not speak and even
as he watched she vanished.
Slowly he knew his arms furred
with a fragrant green darkness
and as the moon cut its swaths
on the ground, as trucks rooted
along the road of colored pleasures,
he felt his feet pushing through
his shoes, his hair went stiff.
He could hear her laugh, could see
her long finger loop a man's ear.
But this did not matter. Already
he felt himself sway a little
in the desert wind, in the wordless
gnarling he became and knew then.

Black Widow

I imagine her trying, trying to catch it. First,
dusting dutifully, but slowed by the child
leaning heavily under her dress, she finds
the web behind her hand loom. Her stalled
hands mean to weave a birth cloth, but surprise
her with another shape. On her face, the worst

black memory crawls near and squats and waits.
She bends, touches her loom to discovery.
The black spot hunches in the black heart
of the corner, snoozing in maternal revery.
Her hands now shake. The web gleams like art.
She feels her heaviness, her blood going to paste.

An hour watching steadies her pulse: she kneels
with the glass jar and makes an awkward strike.
Legs black as a satin dinner dress uncoil
and dance her back in memory to moves quick
in her body's dream. Clumsy, afraid, she fails
again – then succeeds, and screws tight the seal.

But punches a small hole for air. All afternoon
she keeps it in the freezer, admiring
that perfect beauty she cannot dispatch.
Home from work, the husband, I find the thing
dead I am supposed to kill. She won't watch.
In the yard the sun squeals. The sky bleeds blue.

We speak about small things, the future slips past.
She piles clothes in a discard box. I hold her,
driven to distance by the swollen bulb
of her womb, but she cries and shivers.
At night she wakes from a dreamed world
poisonously spinning, claiming her girlish waist

explodes, my foot on it like an executioner. She
swears she's full of spiders, still half
asleep, and kicks the blankets off to lie
naked in a little glow like an hourglass.
Accused, I roll in the sheets as if to hide
in my own dark the fear of what she bears and flees.

August, on the Rented Farm

In this season, through the clear tears
of discovery, my son calls me
to an abandoned barn. Among
spiders' goldspinning and the small
eulogies of crickets, he has entered
the showering secret of our lives,
and the light fur of something
half-eaten mats his hands.
Later, on a rotting length
of pine, we sit
under the star-brilliance
of birds fretting the light.
Under them, dreamless,
we have come to cast
our lot with songs
of celebration.
All afternoon we sit and become
lovers, his hand in mine
like a bird's delicate wing.
Everywhere sparrows go down
to the river for the sweet
tears of communion. Soon,
in the yellow last light,
we will begin again to speak
of that light in the house
that is not ours, that is only
what we come to out of the fields
in the slow-plunging knowledge
of words trying to find a way home.

Waving

In the backyard, by the stilled
oscillations of the cheap
metal fence defined
by the weight of children,
the small maple
waves in the first
gusts of a fall day.
Behind breath-frosted
glass, hearing far off
my child's cry, I
see this waving become
my father's thick arms.
He waves at the ball game
where players swarm
at his call. One spits.
He waves from the nose
of a rowboat, drunk
with fish, unashamed.
He waves at the black
end of a treeless street
where my mother has turned
from the house, crying.
He waves on a little hill
above the playground,
his whistle shearing
over each knuckle
of asphalt. When I stop
running, out of breath,
he is still there, waving,
and I am waving, beating
the air with my arms,
sore and afraid,
and there is no wind, only
the brilliant distance
like a fence between us,
waving and waving.

A Moment of Small Pillagers

That flock of starlings hewing the air
above the orchard is nothing
but the strangling of desire.
I know their country is nowhere
and would not throw a single stone
against such beautiful longing.
They have walked out to be
at the heart of our bodies,
and cannot find what they want,
or even a gleam from the gone sun.
Under them I bend down quietly
and pick up a black feather
as if it were the dropped scarf
of my sleeping daughter. Holding
this for hours, I find myself
unable to say a simple word
true or false, until I become
the little thing my body is
in the hiding fur of a woods.
Then I look across the hedgerows
at the foreign light of my house.
Somewhere in the distance of dark
a voice is calling my name,
but not too loud, and I want
to fly up and gather the last
radiance of the sun and take it
like a song down to her mouth.
Oh daughter, in the thick trees
where fruit bruises beyond joy,
I hunch among the starlings.

The Dark Eyes of Daughters

Flying from the end of my
boot, my daughter's cat,
and the tame quail gone
up in a spatter of feathers,
to leave me turning there
as the dew dulls out, bare
shoulders flushed from that
quick sprint, the back door
still banging like a flattened
wheel of memory. I think
I can hear the world grind.
I feel like a man in a car
who's just dropped something
barely alive on a quiet street.
I am saying *Please, please*
and only mean I want to go
on wherever I am going.
I want the trees to remain
a close forgiving green
without that hot light
ahead banging down hard. I
don't want, for God's sake,
to hear this slow gouging
of sparks that the world is,
the intense unloosening stare
in the cat's eyes as I loom
out of the sudden stillness,
the fixed and believing
pupils of the child startled
to see what cruelty is, always
to know this first dream of
love's division. I am crying
Please, oh please – not
wanting this to happen yet,
sun the color of a cat falling
on her struck face that is
learning to mouth these words
without end, with only one

beginning already long lost
like pawprint or feather
where grass goes stunningly
dead and pain, like flint, strikes.

Pine Cones

Any way you hold them, they hurt.
What's the use, then?

Once in our backyard, by a sparrow's hidden
tremor there in the green wish of spruce,
a full but unfolded body hung.

It bore every color of the world and was sweet
beyond measure. The canyon wind banged
at this then went elsewhere.

Something happened that night.
The sparrow seems to have seen what it was.

Look at him huddled, mistakably some other shadow,
the sly outlines of his body almost blue as spruce,
the sun like a big wall nearby

and you stepping through it, big, so big
he would almost give up his only wish.

Almost. Almost. Almost.

Isn't this the way hearts beat in the world,
the way pine cones fall in the night
until they don't?

When you pick them up, as children do,
the tiny spot appears in your palm,
red as the sun's first blink
of love.

And that sticking, unabidable tar.

Rain Forest

The green mothering of moss knits shadow and light,
the silence and call of each least bird where
we walk and find there are only a few words
we want to say: water, root, light, and love,
like the names of time. Stunned from ourselves
we are at tour's tail end, our guide long gone,
dawdling deep in what cannot be by any human
invented, a few square miles of the concentric
universe intricate as the whorls of fingertips.
The frailest twigs puff and flag in the giantism
of this elaborate grotto, and we are the dream,
before we know better, of an old grotesque
stonecutter who squats under a brow of marble.
We have entered the huge inward drift behind
his eyes and wait to become ourselves. We stare
through limpid eyes into the vapor-lit past
where breath, wordlessly, like a near river
seams up, seams in and out around darkness.
Somewhere far back in the hunch of shadows,
we stood by this wall of vines, and he, angry,
froze us in our tracks and the blade of belief.
That tree there bore the same long slithering
of light from a sky he owned. Disfigured now,
its trunk rises thick and black as a monument
that rings when struck. Here the hiking path,
a crease, stops, then spirals around into stumps.
Our party has gone that way, stumbling quietly.
From time to time, someone calls out but we know
only the words whispered from the wall of leaves:
water, root, light, and love. We stand silent
in the earliest air remembered, hearing at last
the distant and precise taps of the mallet
until our clothes, as if rotted, fall away
and the feckless light fixes us on the column
of our spines. Without warning, we begin to dance,
a bird cries, and another. Our feet seem to spark
on the hard dirt as we go round the black tree
and for no reason we know we see ourselves

throwing our heads back to laugh, our gums
and teeth shiny as cut wood, our eyes marbled,
straining to see where it comes from, that
hoarse rasp of joy, that clapping of hands
before which we may not speak or sing or ever stop.

In the Yard, Late Summer

In the yard the plum tree, wild
with a late summer wind,
shakes its thousand planets
of sweet flesh.
Does it mean to resist
this gush that drops
one order of things
into another? It keels,
leaning at forces we can't
see, can't know the edge of.
Its memory keeps only two
commands: this lives, not
this in the licking sun.
There is no metaphor
to reveal what it has known
in its brooding years.
We watch the purple fruit fall
as leaves shear and snap
and nail themselves to light.
Between us the wind
is a word seeking a shape,
hovering in passion
and risen from the ground
of memory clenched
in long roots and tendrils.
Hearing that, knowing ourselves
wingless and bestial, we wait
for the sun to blow out,

for the return of that first
morning of pink blossoms
when we saw the dark stains
of our feet printing
what we were on that
dew-bed of the world.
The tree, too, waits
in its old unraveling
toward a naked silence,
its language keening, shocked.

FROM **HOMAGE TO EDGAR ALLAN POE**

(1981)

Halloween Delight

Blue apple of the night,
apple of fear,
apple of peace,
the small leaves tear
and hiss in their fright
and the big moon screams

in its rut of the darkness.
Why is it hung there
on the starred rug
like a toy you hear
broken and distant? Why shrug
so? Have you not been blessed?

The boy who was once a man
thinks of no question
as he stands blued
by the dark that beckons.
He lifts his hand
and blots out the moon.

You have done this, long ago.
Perhaps you remember.
And recall that toy
now, and a night off far
watching apples as a boy.
They dance in the wind-blow.

Surely, you thought, by light
all will be torn.
And the leaves were, but
the apple held, shorn
as your heart's delight
nakedly crying Where? Why? What?

Only what is never answered,
nor ever is why.
Stand there and watch.
Small leaves rip and die
at home. Like love's speech.
Lift your hand, go on. Remember.

Bluejays

She tries to call them down,
quicknesses of air.
They bitch and scorn,
they roost away from her.

It isn't that she's brutal.
She's just a girl. Worse,
her touch is total.
Her play is dangerous.

Darkly they spit each at each,
from tops of pine and spruce.
Her words are shy and sweet,
but it's no use.

Ragged, blue, shrill,
they dart around like boys.
They fear the beautiful
but do not fly away.

Desks

Piled on a loading dock where I walked,
    student desks battered, staggered
by the dozens, as if all our talk
    of knowledge was over,

as if there'd be no more thin blondes
    with pigtails, no math, no art,
no birds to stare at. Surplus now, those molds
    we tried to sleep in, always hard

so it wouldn't be pleasant and we'd fall
    awake in time for the one question
with no answer. Quiet as a study hall,
    this big place, this final destination,

oblivious of whatever the weather is,
    hearing the creak of the wind's weight.
The desks are leg-naked, empty, as if
    we might yet come, breathless, late.

And all that time I thought of the flames
    I hadn't guessed, of a blonde
I had loved for years, how the names
    carved one into another would

all scar out the same, blunt, hard, in blue
    searing, like love's first pain.
I stood there like a child, scared, new,
    bird-eyed, not knowing why I came.

Pond

The soft forgiving ooze of the pond's bottom,
that cool fluid move through the toes
when you step out just beyond roots,
through weeds, into that black slough

that the dream has warned is love's terror:
to stand in this abiding rut among shells
born of ancestors, bearing the future,
is to feel all the flesh in the world

and to think of the last time you were in love,
the vertigo, the skidding infinite sky,
the lily's perfect, opening moves,
that slippery reek, that quick eternity.

Homage to Edgar Allan Poe

1. *The Hygeia Hotel: Old Point Comfort*

When I was six grandparents brought me here in a Hudson
green as the swamps of the Chesapeake.

We passed the gates of Fort Monroe to the sea-wall.
With string and a fresh chicken neck
I tried for the great Blue Crab.

They walked the promenade before the towering hotel.
Their war was over.
Now and then I might see them
gathered in knots, men in strange brown suits,
women holding pastel skirts that bloomed in the wind.

Like flowers they swayed, smudged with tears.
That was 1948. I was impatient to go.
Once, holding hands, we went up the wide gray stairs.

Waiters scurried, white silk shirts, black pants.
Through tight lips they spoke softly.
The candles held all dim,
as if the war kept on.

Later, we watched the Bay Line's steamer *Pocahontas*
glide away north to Baltimore.

Tonight steamed crabs are in the air and the moon
and mud's black flesh come forth at low tide.
Here, in 1849, Miss Ingram of Norfolk
heard Poe read 'Ulalume'.

In three days he would die screaming on a table,
the poet possessed by the slosh and slime
of America. She wrote:

'There were many persons on the long verandas
that surrounded the hotel, but they seemed
remote and far away.'

In the Hudson going home that night, I was buried
between the old ones, their bodies ripe.
Around us night congealed.

Ahead, the steady toss of the Chesapeake. Headlights
clawed the dark. I was too small to see much,
frightened by the voice on the radio

declaiming 'The Shadow Knows'.

2. *Nekkid*

                    Why was I there?
Fourteen, lank, moody, marked
by appetites that seeped up like convictions
in parents, shipped to summer camp near Richmond,

I wasn't Robbie or Bill, his drowned brother.
I would not launch myself stark *nekkid*
from the sycamore, however summer blistered,
however girls in canoes cheered,
however welcome might be the hole
of the James River.

I sucked in my Poe, suffered, at near anything flared,
thus was let alone, as weird.

Wearing black jeans, T-shirt, boots, I climbed beyond
a ragtop Ford parked, past an old wooden bridge
plodded in my sweat along a path
that took me one morning clear

to a humped outcrop of bare stone with a view
of the valley, the river, and Poe's city.
                              Below,
curves, mounds, swelling distances straight down.

I edged out by inches, as if to the lip of truth,
daring death or fate, and stripped to my chest
and shouted at the depths.
Unanswered, I backed up, afraid of the fall,

but saw Richmond erect over its cobblestoned streets.
From windows slaves framed in the air
the sun piked back
out of warehouses and wharves,
the prison, taverns, the sleeping rooms of whores,

so I imagined. Easy to believe Poe came from this.
In my mind a manly city, state, what I wanted,
not my maze of green, long days with guides
droning the names of leaves.
What did I know of sap rising in veined hollows?

I climbed because I wanted to *see*,
and not just the close-lapping slit
of the river you wallow in and never know.
I wanted to look at the whole spread-eagled beauty,
the thick pollution of foam
spit along the pink bumps and archipelagos.

I knew that down there the boys went nekkid
and I would sometime, maybe.
                                        Robbie's brother

told me it would be like swimming to the bottom,
your toes pushing from that muck,
eyes closed, trying to feel
your way headfirst to the air.
Then you'd scream. And you'd stink.

Climbing down with hunger to those I'd left bobbing
slick in the shallow pools, somewhere
from a socket of leaves
I heard it –
                    that scoring wheeze of the flesh.
I stopped, uncertain, shadowed, still
hearing Robbie's brother's
imitation, maybe.

Her legs waved naked across his back.
As pale as I was, he buried himself in her
while I watched her face roll toward me and wink.
She grinned, whispered, while he plunged, near

enough I seemed to *feel* his shout:

'You dead son of a bitch!'

I ran certain this meant my throat cut,
busting through bush, my body ripping vines loose
that brought blood, and wasn't caught.
Unless you count nights lying awake, shaken, hoping
each rumor of footstep or leaf-fall meant
she had come to call me into darkness.

Unless you count that appalling, grinning face
I carted home the summer I passed through Richmond,
a face as hopeless as the bridge I clattered over,
far more than nekkid
as lost as Robbie's drowned brother.

Unless you count the wishing I was not
weird, not in love with her wink,
and not a son of a bitch
to be flung like spit into the universe.

3. *Nightcrawlers*

I thought of an old crabber, a figure draining his bottle,
tossing it as he trolled in toward the pier
lit up yellow, late, lonely.

His hands tying down the 24 foot scow would seem to glow,
(as if he was holy flesh, I almost wrote)
black crabs bubbling in the barrel.

Under stars glowing like a small town sitting to supper,
I took off my shoes and walked again. Was he
invented, scowling, raw-faced?

Black summer grass, and wet, took me through sandyards
where people coaxed roses, and crawlers lugged.
Squashed as I stepped. *Phrenologists call it*

Veneration, Poe wrote. I stood near the wharf's bobbing,
shunting hulls for whoever might come. Water,
gasoline slicked, seemed alive with worms.

In my poems I had made him hard-shelled, possessed,
like Edgarpoe, battler with seas, mystic eye.
This one was fat and clumsy

as he wedged the deadrise hull to its slip, pots, tools,
crabs sent atumble, shuddering, the rest flung
down the gullet of her wheelhouse.

No word between us heroic or miserable. It passed,
that grunt of a face going home, sneakers
squishing as he hefted his catch.

As regards the greater truths, men oftener err by
seeking them at the bottom than at the top.
Can the imagination lie? Then, what good?

All I found was this local genius, the tired
heave of him dark as flounder eyes
where the kitchen table was set.

She put the crab meat white as swan feathers before him.
His platter steamed under the grace he spoke.
I thought of Poe, womanless, wormy.

She kissed lightly the old one's salted neck, and sank
beside him while he ate, both
exhausted, luminous.

4. *A Dream of Poe Hiding Out in New York*

Worked over here by critics, I was screwed.
2am, I leave the bar and walk as a man
in need of a woman. She comes, who's
inescapable, and no bargain.

Working off the smell of them, that's the problem.
First touch light, soon greasy.
The street glistening like phlegm.
more rain plummeting.

                    Almost, it washes you
clean, so sudden and total is it.
In an X-rated theater I take refuge.
The screen is filled with tits.

I always think of Helen, my dove.
Skittery as sleet.
Naked, like sleet. But love
and flesh are different. Flesh reeks.

The light in here is blue.
It blinds you like history. The twist
is it gets the blood up for Truth.
Truth left me beshit

in Baltimore, sodden, and stunned.
I've tried to forget years of their pleas,
little hands, tongues, women
just dried blood now. But she,

the late and best loved one, renews
me when I come here, that rivet
of nerves below, the brute
bed-dent we made. I forget

without these visual aids that I am
Poe, poet, addict and dreamer.
Or is the world scum?
Blood flecks her lips in slumber.

Walking late I watch the lewd
movies, with dark am conversant.
All speaks to me of what I might do
to affront the black moment.

And what is that say you?
Keep an innocence eternal as New York.
Where Death is no great virtue,
it is merely perfect.

Yet who in pit, sty, or mausoleum
wants it? *You do, honey.*
Then, foul bitch, make me human.
Do it. Screw me.

5. *The End of Everything*

How it glints out where least expected, the pink
spread of dawn light in clots of ice

where the milk-horse of the past always broke through
night's crust. I have risen with air in my throat

blooming, shouldering up its white stalk. My love, lying
behind me in a fragrant bed, remarks how precious

is 'the shining body of the world'. And there, greasy,
over the windowsill, the mushrooming first light

(red as bougainvillaea) silently crawls the naked street
where the horse once stood huffing, nearly invisible,

its spine enough to shatter starlight, a jeweler's blade
cracking loose a final fire. Look at it running

in the wheel's ruts, a pulse intermittent, ectoplasmic.
Like the wings of Pegasus beating themselves to dust.

Now on elbows, keeping my nightmarish face outside
the room where she stirs to silk, I speak of the great

pink-orange orchid of the future, serenely, soundlessly
sucking our breath to its bloom above the manure piles.

6. *Steamer to Baltimore*

Tonight we are watching the stars at the bow,
our heads draped over, giddy with blood,
body and boat drifting in another sky.
We think of Poe, the American, riding Chesapeake
channels inward with wind-fret where seahawks
blink like critics in cordgrass.
                              He believed
in the perfect eyes of love that wait
beyond the deep rotting of time. We
have ridden out in a rib-thudding scow

to feel where his dream flows. Look at us
lining the rail, moons the tide floats past,
each one Edgarpoe, longing for home.
This is the pilgrim's road to Baltimore.
The engines churn, the raked hull broods.

Portrait of a Lady

October, that glittering rakehell month,
snorts in the bushes where the widow is
busy with weeds. They still defeat her.
With them she has trafficked for years,
but what if she, puttering, with rake,
with shears, should suddenly discover
her fingers have gone numb? On knees
bent, face lifted so the black streaks
of earth seem time's batterings, she
may yet remember the high shrill stars
at the edge of summer and sing, for
behind them a darkness not earth parts
gently again and again. And if, then,
her brow in light sweat breaks to wear
the mask that runs to mud along bone,
let us lean close and watch and hear her
work as deep as ever through the hours.
She was beautiful once and may be again.
In October the leaves are lipped in ice
but heat, like hope, lingers in flowers,
under nails, in the cleaving song she sings.

Waking Under a Spruce With My Love

Up the hill the motorcycle climbs, its growl
near now, entering my dream,
and the girl's hair flares

because it's morning, because I have been sleeping
long enough to become one of the muscles
flexed with the world's gristle.

I can feel the sheet luff on my thighs, the emptiness
cool and pleasant inside my body, and time
stops counting the spruce limbs.

I think this must be the silence that love wants to be,
except I can hear a dog barking, a big dog
far away, then his nails gouging dirt,

and I feel myself twist for the power to get free.
The little engine pumps hard, she hangs
on my shoulders, and we are not

going down in grinding of gravel, not this time, we
are filling silence with the two-stroke slide
of the morning and time rattles

like joy in the spruce, in the car-door slammed, jays
spitting out the black, stale hours,
the sun flying over each bump

in the road, touching the essence of each thing until
the world ticks, sighs, glides ahead easy,
slows, turns, and comes hard again.

Elk Ghosts: A Birth Memory

Tirelessly the stream licks the world until
from snow they do not come, but are
hoof-deep and standing, silhouettes
stark on the stones under stars.

Gathered, they seek a way to reenter
paths graven on the bone-walls.
Their white breath is alive. It is
possible to walk into and out

of monstrous, gentle eyes, knowing no link
exists except your face anchored
in the herd's dream. They are beyond
stillness and memory, their

revelation the lapping fire-fleck of water
and the starbright lintel of stones.
They come here to wait for change,
to be dreamed among pine and spruce.

There is no hawk who could hook them
out of the blue they breathe
effortlessly. Each moon-swollen
needle leads them more into vision.

Time conspires with you at night's window
and cannot help but hope for this
birth of joy. No longer do they
wait, no more nuzzle the future.

They glide through desire on earth.
Their thin song has entered each reed,
it has risen in your sleep and wails
forth these white shadows

you have summoned. They become electric
in your blood. One after another
they bear the stars, walking on water,
beasts with backs of pure light.

There is no world they cannot carry.
They are love's magi. Hooves flare
with a way through the darkness.
Composed, they suffer your coming.

Wedding Song

Camden, North Carolina, is not picturesque
though it is the place we remember
where many men and women have gone
in good luck and bad to repair
aching hearts: for five dollars
no one asks your age or looks for the curve

swelling under the skirt of the cheerleader.
Our justice of the peace pumped gas
and spoke the words through gums
long toothless and tobacco black.
A tourist honked for help.

He gave each of us a sample box of Cheer.
Y'all come on back anytime!

The first time down Route 17, by George Washington's
ditch, he of the chopped cherries,
we turned back in the Dismal Swamp.
Who could make up a truer thing than that?

You weren't fooling. Neither was I.
The second time we made it.

A wheezing clerk above an X-rated movie house
slowly printed our names.
He chewed an onion's golden rings.
He said *Are you now or have you ever been crazy?*

Weren't we? Isn't love something that breaks,
drooling and dangling inside
like a car's hot-water hose
that leaves you helpless,
godforsaken in the middle of nowhere?

Y'all come on back anytime.
Fifty bucks and two economy boxes of Cheer –
how far could we get on that?

I was certain you'd end up croaking home
to mother after those early months.

Our first house had more holes
than we could cover, mice,
snakes, spiders, our dinner guests.

In that place you woke to the screams of a mare
who dropped half of her foal, dragging
half around the rented house until
with tractor and chain
the landlord delivered us.

The chain still dangles in your dreams,
and his *Y'all come back anytime.*

Sometimes when I think we have learned
to live in the world, the faces
of children lining our walls,
the darkness waiting ahead
like a swamp that's no joke,

I turn and find you coiled in a corner of light.
I think of the five green dollars unfurled
for that clerk of hunger and fools,
the blue acrid soap
that scoured us cherry red,
and the screams of our years.

Are we now or were we ever crazy?
Sign here, the man said, and we did,

the voices of men and women
making love, cracking up
through that black movie floor.

I hear them still.

Reading the Books Our Children Have Written

They come into the room while quail are crying to huddle up,
canyon winds just beginning. They pass my big brown desk,
faces damp and glistening as freshly washed peaches,
and offer themselves to be kissed. Everything's father,
I kiss them, I say *See you tomorrow!* Their light steps
fade down stairs, what they are saying like the far stars
shrill, hard to understand. They try to say how a father
writes his book, how they are in it, who are his loves.
Then in their beds they wait for sleep, sometimes singing.

Later I get up and go down in darkness to find the hour
before they were scrubbed, before they brought me new faces.
There on the floor I find stapled pages, the mild, strange
countenances of animals no one has ever seen, the tall man
who writes an endless story of those homeless in the night.
They have numbered each page and named each colorful wing.
They have done this to surprise me, surprising themselves.
On the last yellow page one has written: *This is a poem.*
Under this the other one's crayon answers: *See tomorrow!*

FROM **DREAM FLIGHTS**
(1981)

Elegy in an Abandoned Boatyard

...mindful of the unhonoured dead
THOMAS GRAY

Here they stood, whom the Kecoughtan first believed
gods from another world, one pair of longjohns
each, bad-yellow, knotted with lice,
the godless, bandy-legged runts
with ear bit off, or eye gouged,
                who killed and prayed
over whatever flew, squatted, or swam.

In huts hacked from mulberry, pine, and swamp cyprus,
they huddled ripe as hounds.
At cockcrow scratched, shuffled paths,
took skiffs and ferried to dead-rise scows,
twenty-footers of local design and right draft
for oysters, crabs, and croakers.
                    They were seaworthy.

According to diaries hand-scrawled,
and terse court records,
our ancestors: barbarous, habitual, Virginians.

Some would not sail, came ashore, walked on the land,
kept faces clenched, lay seed and family,
moved often, and are gone. Of them
this harbor says nothing.

Of the sea's workmen, not much,
no brass plate of honor, no monument in the square,
no square, merely the wreckage of a place.
                    But they stood –

proud, surly in mist at the hovel of the boatwright,
the arm pointed: *Build me one like that yonder!*
Meaning the hull I see bottom up in ashen water,

nameless now as themselves, except to the squat one
known to crush clams in his palms, our kin,
the boatwright. He gave credit to each son,

barring feud, and took stick in hand
to dig from earth the grave first line of a keel,

who often would lift his brow seaward, unspeaking,
until a shape buried in air hove up
and he made it become what they wanted,
                              Like that one yonder!

This was all the image for tomorrow he would give us,
each boat a little different, the best guess
changed to meet the sea's change
of rot and stink and silence.
To make hulls he knew
to be riddles, feasts for worms,
he came into this world even as I now have
entered his place to sit at the charred last log.
Only when I begin to hear the lies
he allowed each to invent
can I feel the hugeness of his belief. Then
I take up a cap left as worthless, drifted

here by god knows what current, sand-pinned,
and feel the plain cast of a broken stick
pulse down my arm like the sun's
hook in a man's brain. So I
                              see it,
                                   immense shadow
on water.
              My eyes squint,
                         and there it is,
                              the wind cradle
of the Eagle's wings, unfurled,
as it might be for men,
even the least, riding the updraft,
unfettered as a dream of change,

                    except somewhere the nest screeching,
the unborn who need more than our dreams
of first wreckage, of last hopes. Where is
he, the one who knew us all, floaters and sinkers,
who brought my fathers here, put my back
against this fallen trunk, let me

pull my stick in the dirt
to make keel and sail?
                                        Digging, I see
my line man-shaped and flight-worthy, a language
the boatwright spoke in this place, all
looking for it to rise and loom,
the boat like the soul
that would bear us hence,
out of the water that beats in,
out of the water that bore us all here.

The Tire Hangs in the Yard

1.

First it was the secret place where I went to dream, end
of the childhood road, deep-tracked, the dark
behind my best friend's house, blackberry
thickets of darkness, and later where
we stared, with willing girls, into the sky.

Past that hedgerow, past fields turned to houses, past
the crows we shot in our bored pleasure, I drive
bathed by green dashlight and the sun's blood
glinting on leaves just parted, then see

again the road's dead-end in woods, its deep stillness
ticking like throat-wheeze – and Jesus Christ
look at the beer cans, the traffic, even
hung on a berry vine somebody's rubber,

and wouldn't you know it that tire still hangs.

2.

On the Churchland Baptist Church the hot ivy hung, smelled
of dust, our mouths lifting their black holes
like a tire I kept dreaming. Clenched
by mother and father who stank sweetly in sweat,

I sang and sang until the black ceiling
of our house seemed to sway and crack
and the tire skulled against my eyes
in time with the great clock in the far hall.

Hanging in darkness, like sex, it made me listen.

3.

One summer night here I came to fistfight Jim Jenrett,
whose house she had gone to, who is now no more
than a frail hand remembered on cheek, and I
was beer-brave, nearly wild with all
the dozen piling from cars. Jesus,
look at us in the ghost-flare of headlights,
pissing, taunting, boy-shadows, me hung
in the tire of my best friend spitting final threats.

So we passed, blinded, into the years, into the trees
holding their scars, half-healed, into the dark
where Jim, dunned by our words, went out
near dawn and stepped in the tire
and shied up the electric extension cord, noosed,
by the rope whose tire, burdened, ticked slowly.

4.

Ghost-heart of this place, of dreams, I give you a shove
and sure enough I hear the tick and all that was
is, and a girl straightening her skirt walks
smack against you and screams. You know
who laughs, smoking in the shadows, don't you?

There are no headlights now, only the arc of blackness
gathering the hung world in its gullet. Blink
and maybe he's there, his great feet jammed
halfway in the hole of your heart,
gone halfway.

5.

Where do they go who were with us on this dream road,
who flung themselves like seed under berry-black
nights, those faces black-clustered,
who could lead down and tell us
what love is and mercy and why now

I imagine a girl, mouth open in the sexual O, her hair
gone dull as soap scum, the husband grunting
as his fist smacks again, her scream
not out yet, nor the promise
she could never love anyone else.

I climb in the tire, swinging like a secret in the dark
woods surrounded by homelights of strangers.
She swore she loved me best.

In the church I imagined this place left forever behind
but it's with me as I try to see the road begin.
Blackberries on both sides blackly hang.
Trees, in blackness, leaned down at me.
When will they come, the headlights
washing over me like revelation,
the cars ticking and swirling like souls?

Once when my mother could not find me, they came here.
They said, 'So this is it, the place.' It was dark,
or nearly, and they said I might have died.
I asked them what being dead was like.
Like swinging at night, they joked, in the trees.

I shove my foot at the dirt, lifting off in blackness.
The whine of the rope is like a distant scream.
I think, so this is it. Really it.

The Pornography Box

At eighteen, the U.S. Navy eye chart
memorized, reciting what was unseen,
my father enlisted for the duration.
At nineteen he caught a casual wave
wrong off Norfolk, our home, called
Hell by sailors. The landing craft
cast him loose and burst his knee.
He lived, and wore his rigid brace
without complaint, and never in this
life showed anyone his secret medal.
I stumbled into that brace and more
when I climbed to our sealed attic
the year a drunk blindsided him
to death in a ditch, and me to love.

Today I watch my ten-year-old son race
over the faultless pages of *Playboy*,
ashamed I brought it home, imagining
his unasked questions have answers.
I remember the chairs I stacked
and climbed, the brace I put on
to see how it felt and, buried
deep in his sea chest, the livid
shapes shoved so far in a slit
of darkness a man could reach them
only hunched, on all fours. I clawed
through families of clothes discharged,
boxed ornaments for Christmas, to feel
the spooky silk of webs slickly
part on my face where blood rushed.

Trussed on their wide bed, my mother lay
surviving wreckage, stitched back
beyond secrets I hadn't guessed yet.
I shimmied through a dark hole
in the ceiling and listened to pine
rake the roof like a man's shuffle.
But he was dead, the box unlocked.

His flashlight pulsed through my body,
each glossy pose burning my eyes
that knew only airbrush innocence.
Sex rose in me like a first beard.
A woman with painted nails peels
a foreskin, another held a man
kingly rigid at her tongue's tip.
I could not catch my breath.

I blinked at one spread on a table's
lace, grandmotherly clean and white.
Here might have been service for tea,
dainty cups, bread, a dish of cakes,
except she was in their place, child
in a middy suit. Behind her a vase
of daisies loomed, the parlor wall
sang *Home, Sweet Home* in needlepoint.
She might have been my young sister.
I remember the eyes, direct and flat,
as if she had died. Stockings knuckled
at her knees, her plaid skirt neatly
rolled on her chest. He, in three-piece
suit, cradled her calves in furred hands,
and placid as a navigator looked out
a window. He entered her like a knife.

After school, at night, weekend afternoons,
I raced to see them do it, legs cramped
in that freezing slot of darkness, gone
wobbly as a sailor into the country.
I came and went in the black tube
death opened for me like a new horizon.
In one sequence a black man held a pool
cue to a white woman, a black woman
grasped, grinning, black and white balls.
The uniforms of sailors were scattered,
wadded everywhere I looked. I smelled
the mothballs from my father's chest
when late at night I woke to vomit
at the clock's slit-eyed glowing.

90

How long does it go on, throbbing dreams,
waking obsessed with a hole in the air?
In Norfolk, from loaded cars, we spilled
at sailors passing alleys, asked for girls,
beer, good times, our cruel sucker-punch
a game played for strangers. *Bye-bye,
Seafood*, we yelled, then headed down
toward the Gaiety Theater and whores
bright as moths. We spit at mothers who
screamed *Fuck you, kid!* Crew-cut, clean,
the secrets of our fathers, we cruised
those hopeless streets shiny as razors.
Neon flared like pus where they laughed
because we wanted love. Seeing now
my son bent to see I imagine at last

my father climbing before me in blackness,
with the tiny light a man carries, bent
on pained knees where I knelt also at
nameless images we each live to love
and fear. Exotics of the ordinary, one
dancer's crinolines flare around her
shaven rose. Another cooks in high heels,
a classmate suddenly gone from our town.
One on a patio reclines, not hiding her
one shorter leg. Each grins and burns
into memory, speaking in shy whispers,
all born to teach us what violation is.
At eighteen what fathers teach is wrong,
for the world is wrong, and only women
know why, their eyes dark as flat seas.

But it isn't eyes sons remember, blinded
by daylight on that raw breast, a thigh
where no face should be so open but is,
and is the mouth of the world's flesh
radiant in its rottenness, the secret
that leaves finally apart and other
all who learn to dream. In memory
I see how each nipple, cleft, face,
touch hissed our shame when accidentally
I became the boy-father of our house,

owner of obscenities. I hated us.
What else is the world but a box,
false-bottomed, where the ugly truths
wait and sail in the skins of ancestors?

Escaping them at last I left for worlds
unknown, but climbed first to his gifts,
carted that box and brace graveside,
and spilled those sweet faces down
under the tall Baptist spire. I spread
gasoline where we put him, then his
Navy Zippo lighter snapped it off.
Quick bodies coiled and flamed, ash
flecks rising like souls before me.
I gouged the remains in a trench
of churchly dirt, tried once to spit,
and turned in the dark for a bus.
In warm sun, his pea-coat was black
as the sea at midnight but I took it,
wore it, sweating for the cold to come.

Women smiled as if I was ripe, flushed
with cash from months at sea. *Welcome,
Anchor-clanker. We've waited for you.*
I was free, I thought, discharged from
Hell into the world that, for Christ's
sake, wanted me. Home was gone, mother
drifting for a life. Maybe I'd write.
But was, after all, busy, holed up
with a nameless girl, the sharp blade
of her body a memory I still carry,
that darling who took my coat. But
by Easter I was ready, went. House sold,
mother maybe married, maybe in Florida,
they said. I wandered in cool sea winds,
as if on shore leave, until I came

cast up where my father was. Posters
of the nailed Jesus littered the grass.
A few crones kneeled faceless as stones
as if to serve the sun dying already.
I shivered, heard traffic hiss, walked

the old roads toward the shipyard and
wished I had our goddamn lost coat.
Boys yelled at me but no one stopped.
Freed, I felt myself. Who understands?
Hours I went in hard ways, night ahead,
my early beard bristling, dreaming what
feathers learn. I came to a seedy hovel,
where films of flesh bared everything.
Among sailors I, a man, heard the siren
call us forward to sit with the heroes
under reels of lighted, loving women,
to dream in a theater called Art's House.
At love's edge, unbraced like my father,
I was nineteen, ready to take my step.

So we went in.

The Colors of Our Age: Pink and Black

That year the war went on, nameless, somewhere,
but I felt no war in my heart,
not even the shotgun's ba-bam
at the brown blur of quail.
I abandoned brothers and fathers,
the slow march through marsh
and soybean nap where
at field's end the black shacks
noiselessly squatted under strings
of smoke. I wore flags of pink:
shirts, cuff links, belt, stitching.
Black pants noosed my ankles
into scuffed buck shoes.
I whistled Be-Bop-A-Lula
below a hat like Gene Vincent's.
My uniform for the light, and girls.

Or one girl, anyway, whose name I licked
like candy, for it was deliciously
pink as her sweater. Celia,
slow, drawling, and honey-haired,
whose lips hold in the deep mind
our malignant innocence of joy.
Among my children, on the first
of October, I sit for supper,
feet bare, tongue numb with smoke,
to help them sort out my history's
hysterical photographs. In pink
hands they take us up, fearless,
as we are funny and otherworldly.

Just beyond our sill two late hummingbirds,
black and white, fight for the feeder's
red, time-stalled one drop.
They dart in, drink, are gone,
and small hands part before me
an age of look-alikes, images
in time like a truce-wall
I stare over. The hot, warping
smell of concrete comes, fear
bitter as tear gas rakes
a public parking lot. Midtown
Shopping Center, Portsmouth, VA.,
the *Life* caption says, ink
faded only slightly, paper yellowing.

Everyone is here, centered, in horror
like Lee Oswald's stunned Ranger.
A 1958 Ford Victoria, finned,
top down and furred dice hung,
seems ready to leap in the background.
The black teenager, no name given,
glares at the lens in distraction.
Half-crouched, he shows no teeth,
is shirtless, finely muscled,
his arms extended like wings.
White sneakers with red stars
make him pigeon-toed, alert.

His fingers spread at his thighs
like Wilt Chamberlain trying
to know what moves and not look.

Three girls lean behind him, *Norcom H.S.*
stenciled on one who wears a circle
pin, another a ring and chain.
Their soft chocolate faces appear
glazed, cheeks like Almond Joys.
They face the other side, white,
reared the opposite direction,
barbered heads, ears, necks.
In between, a new shiny hammer
towers like an icon lifted
to its highest trajectory.
A Klan ring sinks into flesh,
third finger, left hand,
cuddling the hammer handle.

This man's shirt is white, soiled,
eagle-shaped, and voluminous. Collar up.
Each detail enters my eye like grit
from long nights without sleep.
I might have been this man, risen,
a small-town hero gone gimpy
with hatred of anyone's black eyes.
I watch the hummingbirds feint
and watch my children dismiss them,
focusing hammer and then a woman
tattooed under the man's scarred
and hairless forearm. The scroll
beneath the woman says *Freedom.*
Above her head, in dark letters
shaped like a school name on
my son's team jacket: *Seoul, 1954.*
When our youngest asks 'Was that
black man the enemy?' I try
to answer: just a soldier, a war...

I watch the feeder's tiny eye-round
drop, perfect as a breast
under the sweater of a girl
I saw go down, scuttling
like a crab, low, hands no use
against whatever had come to beat
into her silky black curls.
Her eyes were like quick birds
when the hammer nailed
her boyfriend's skull. Sick,
she flew against Penny's wall,
our hands trying to slap her sane.
In the Smarte Shoppe, acidly,
the mannequins smiled
in disbelief. Then I was
yanked from the light, a door

opened. I fell, as in memory I fall
to a time before that time.
Celia and I had gone to a field,
blanket spread, church done,
no one to see, no one expected.
But the black shack door opened,
the man who'd been wordless
always spoke, his words intimate
as a brother's, but banging out.
He grinned, he laughed, he wouldn't
stop. I damned his lippy face
but too late. He wiggled
his way inside my head.
He looked out, kept looking
from car window, school mirror,
from face black and tongue
pink as the clothes he wore.

Often enough Celia shrieked for joy,
no place too strange or obscene
for her, a child of the South,
manic for the black inside.
When he fell, she squeezed
my hand and more, her lips came
fragrant at my ear. I see them

near my face, past the hammer.
But what do they say? Why, now,
do I feel the insuck of breath
as I begin to run – and from her?
Children, I lived there and wish
I could tell you this is only
a moment fading and long past.

But in Richmond, Charlotte, God knows
where else, by the ninth green,
at the end of a flagstone pathway
under pine shadow, a Buick waits
and I wait, heart hammering,
bearing the done and the undone,
unforgiven, wondering in what
year, in what terrible hour,
the summons will at last come.
That elegant card in the hand
below the seamless, sealed face –
when it calls whoever I am
will I stand for once and not run?
Or be whistled back, what I was, hers?

Out here, supper waiting, I watch my son
slip off, jacketed, time, place,
ancestors of no consequence to him,
no more than pictures a man carries
(unless a dunk shot inscribed).
For him, we are the irrelevance of age.
Who, then, will tell him of wars,
of faces that gather in his face
like shadows? For Christ's sake
look, I call to him, or you will
have to wait, somewhere, with us.
There I am, nearest the stranger
whose hammer moves quicker
than the Lord's own hand. I am
only seventeen. I don't smoke.
That's my friend Celia, kissing me.
We don't know what we're doing.
We're wearing pink and black.
She's dead now, I think.

The Water Horse

1.

We lived in love's house at Bennet's Creek.
The tides were ordinary except once
when we heard the cry of a beast

disappearing: the cry keens back when we touch.
Sea-flooded acres, terrified creatures
swirling, weightless in the black.

2.

In the nightlong twining of our bodies
nothing had told us the earth
slowly vanished with one

mare swimming the railfence. Saddled by mist
the stallion kept himself apart
like a man without love.

3.

A live skin of water, no walkable ground.
The cry was, we saw, her head floating
past, one whose hooves moved

like a crab on what had been meadow, deepness
a new womb. Composed, spirit of power,
black eyes all for him.

4.

I felt his head lift as if at the brain ice
bullets struck, as if below his hooves
the world vanished. What words

say what his nerves heard when he leaped over
an edge for love's house? Sometimes
in your arms I hear him.

5.

Hoof-strikers,

Dawning came and wide water fell.
Your mothers lined the shore.
One cried, out some way, so there
I went in and two of us rose silted
shaggy, glistening in the world.
Everything followed to the field
where misted grasses we ate
grew forever. Then we were fearless.

With water our god washed us clean
to make love breathe. We obeyed
dark's promise. If we had not done this
the earth would not have returned,
the crabs would own everything.
You would have vanished with us.

Cleaning a Fish

In her hand the knife, brisk, brilliant as moon-claw,
shaves the flesh. It grazes the white
belly just over the heart.
Underneath, the coiled fingers
are cradling a soft body
as if it were the jowls of the aged

man propped for a while on the bench in the park.
The head is not severed, the eyes not out.
Blue, they appear to flash odd ways
where a tree makes a live shadow.

Mostly the eyes are dead.
Nothing is in them

except the intense blue of sky the tree allows.
There is no conspiring of nerves,
no least event recalled
by a limb's high arching,
or even a girl's ascension
from a forgotten distance of water.

But there is something as she lifts the meat.
It is enough to draw down her gaze.
Now her arm rises against
yellow hair fallen
white in a childish face.
She is still as a leaf barely clinging.

I come to her like a cat in the stunned grass
and touch her to see the startled,
upthrusted gleam of her brow.
At each cheek and temple
like gathered beads of mist
scales leap with sun, and are dead.

No word passes between us, but something electric
as a flash of steel makes her
cry out just once. Squatting
at the yard's edge, she
sings beyond any thought.
Her knife flies as lethal as love
and cuts quickly in like a hurried kiss.

Wildfire

Crackling like fear in the child's heart late awakened,
the parents have gone into nightmare,
on the lake of darkness
far away are carried, and the house
dreadfully closes.

It smiles like dawn in the wide western window.
No one believes this ever.
But there is glass-flutter.

There is wind hungering and the far sister
of the aspen trying to crawl.

Then it will be seen to leap the ridge distance,
going entirely.
Something has come in the dark, touching.
But the air wonderfully now
is sheepish and light lacquers all.

Snowlight nearly, down,
the singlet of geese travelers,
something like a word from the north,

this wholeness fully breathable
heaping its handful of gray on the ground.
Like mist and fog from a mill town rising
as if the earth had just been
created,

as it has,

and memory's hand opening above the coverlet,
and the family mouth open
and all over.

Tide Pools

At dusk and long distance they are the mouths
to another world, caves of silence that speak
only in light, and tonight, family packed
for home travel, we take a last, slow route
over sand the sea has all day been stroking.
At driftwood the children stop, first veering
off wordlessly, and kneel to know some texture

of change, or stand merely to dream themselves
freely into the gathering shadows of the land.
As we go ahead of them, we imagine their hands
collecting what seems to have waited for each,
shells, starfish, agates sharp as a lover's eye.
Then we also drift apart, each following new
runnels the tide has left, and after a while
I see you hunched on a rock, almost part of it.
The light is nearly gone and the wind chills me
so I think of my father's whistle, ways it called
the sundered shadows of a family into the house.
But I don't whistle now, through the lips he made,
for somehow we have come where we may be apart
and whole. Instead I walk forward to understand
how each one is taken into the shapes of this place.

Then I find it, the deepest pool, its rock-vaulted
light bending as if alive in water faintly moving.
I see the lacy deceivers, the creatures disguised
as rock whose breath flutes in freshets like joy.
A killdeer cries from the black suck of the surf
and, though sweet, that darkness is not wanted.
This hole swells with the sun's final gold
and by it I learn to see what I always suspected –
the little unkillable pulsations of our life.
I gaze into the spooling depths, absorbed by all
that's bottomless, the open shells, the glitter
of hulls laid forever side by side like the dead
unwarily caught at last, perfect and untouchable.
How can I help sinking among those who loved us?

When finally I whistle there is almost no light,
but there's enough. You come then, invisible,
a sound made by the sand, a mingling of laughter,
and I duck under just in time, holding my breath.
Eyes burning, I watch as you bend to find me.
How I love your squeal of delight when I burst
up like a king from underground! Soon we're all
in naked and splashing, flying up like white birds.
The road home will be long and dark, the stars cold,
but collected like this we will be buoyed beyond
the dark snags and splinters of what we once were.

BLUE SPRUCE

(1981)

I.

Shimmering like woman's walk, heartblue of the earth,
suddenly you are there at my window,
and I am miles off, longing.

As if I, unwinged chrysalis, had climbed the last limb's
edge, at the infinite road,
no longer myself,

I take the wind in, and colors, and the keening distance.
Who are you to have called me
out of my stillness,

what voice of fire that melts the ice of memory far back?
Wingsleek, upthrusting power, gate-opener
to the languid meadows of air,

I am with you now, no more than an ash from dark cauldrons
of the sun. Wandering in the blue forms
of your body, I sing

as if nothing can keep me, buoyant as June's new goldfinch.
Who are you that I must fly like this,
in words crying out?

II.

The blue deer leaps out of the spruce,
elegant and fluid
as the mountain spring.

She stands head down, held by the grass,
as the small wind comes,
and her perfumed

limbs drift at my window just opened.
I look harder, beginning
to shape a lost image

out of hooves and delicate shoulders,
a neck subtle as the dawn.
God help me, my sounds

clatter and stumble like a boy's first love.
These are only words, I say,
but already you are gone.

III.

When the blue deer will not leave its home,
when the spruce arms bind up with ice,
though the sun's flare at my window goes,

I put my face like a child's against the glass.
I do not speak now, keeping inside
the fog of my words, hoping to be at last

seen by all that I long for on the other side.
More than once the cold wind's rattler
looses the small flock of sparrows to sky

like pieces of a dream. Each whistle disappears.
I close my eyes to follow them,
circles on circles, hearing what I do not hear.

Returned, they will gather to a single tendon,
heart, tail, hoof, the shy mouth
blue with passion I can never hope to abandon.

IV.

Laboring late, at last I push away from words.
I snap off the lights and then,
yawning at my window where the swirled
snowgleam uncovers all for the great owl

of darkness, I see the spruce easily shudder.
Snow falls like gowns of silk
around the seawave shadow
lovely as a woman who eases herself

toward me, toward the darkness I am keeping.
I open the window with clawed fingers.
Who but you understands? I say.
The blue of her breath in each naked hair

films my house, my country, my children.
Halfway she stops, stamps at ice, shakes her head.

V.

Blue deer, soul of all songs,
Blue spruce, ovoid, rooted,
Blue light of the first hour,
Blue tone, glint in the scale

the yard's rattlesnake rides,
you hear each thing ache to
say what it is. You are always
moving, our name, our body

one in your unfolding silence.
You are like the ripped cry
of desire, the final shiver
at the root of the frog's tongue.

Swallowed, lumps in winter's
hunger. The great void whirls
without us while inside you
we remain, gliding on black

ice of unimagined distances,
stars and limb-knockings. Or
wait, salted in the deep breath
the dead keep for all births.

Then, wordless, without warning,
the wire-white of moonlight
and the insect hum marries.
In you a singing is summoned.

It holds cold torrents of dreams,
and the back tumbled rock,
and the translucent skins,
the wild apple's blue bite.

Spring blisters us to say what
we are: your black hoof, head
shy as love in the glass, all
waiting and swelling and deadly.

VI.

Why is it whenever I step beyond
the window's skin
and enter the yard's distance
to stand near you,
I am myself, and nothing to say?

There is no season to change this.
In winter with snow in sheets
fine as a girl's throat,
I am the shadow in your shadow.
In summer I am the sun's meat.

But in my head I turn to you my one
last glance, without season,
and there you are. Sometimes
just the quick spark of a hoof,
sometimes you nearly enclose me.

Maybe you are only my heart's hiss.
Maybe you are not blue at all.
Blindness of selves, you are
I see not only one. Many,
nothing I have said named you once.

VII.

August, breathless, sun spreading clear
like the ooze of a blister,
grass on itself lying down.

From my window I see the inner motion
that moves it all and bids wanton
birds stand still on their tight claws.

Almost I see the diamonds flash, the raw
tongue's speech, the liquid flow
that enteres the spruce like fate.

My body coils against itself and waits
for the deer's effortless leap.
Why do the limbs so calmly whisper?

Everything beats in passion, even the birds.
I feel their hard eyes shine and dart.
I begin to imagine the sun

boiling through each feather, cell and bone.
I slide over the sill and go
rattling, not myself, some other

loose in the yard where moments ago I dreamt
love was the world, confident,
in a blue hoofstriker's grip.

VIII.

October, the edged wind rousts the dying ground,
whips each blue-laced limb, and the moon
slides like memory across my bed.

Naked as the night's owl, a beast smell, a blue
summons me, it flickers sourceless as fire
in the heart. I rise, a killing tune

on my tongue, and feel the flat taste, as of iron,
spread through all that I am. I see into dark
with nerve's sureness, the great flyer

I am drumming and crooning, more deadly than art.
Above all I circle and look, honed claw,
waiting to plunge down where the spark

of blue flames from a wet small eye like a flaw.
Whatever climbs from an earth tunnel
as if out of itself, I want that quickness raw,

its blood for myself, its skitter of dirt, its squeal.
In this hunting season I most live.
My dive makes a world-play. I must kill

to keep inside what the inner world gives.
I will kill myself in my own good time,
summoned to the sun's ends. There's no help for this.

When I think of those gone already, I smell the plum
I shat them into, the frantic pine swaying
like my spirit. I hit rattlesnakes like a bomb.

How can love and death in such beauty as mine mix?
Orders. Fly in deep blue until dead.
Wind alone tells secrets: fall now, now be lifted.

IX.

There would be no more than this,
the snow-wash trickling down,
the quiet grace of the spruce,
the once birth-wet eyebrow

of white fox gathering a red ice.
Without malice, it came
through the roots of the ash
or out of cave blackness, like flame,

110

fell into the furdrifts of necks.
There was no bristling of teeth,
and little blood on the stalks
drained to gold. No screams

where the moon-splinters would cling
like an odd song, canted, hissed.
Under the fanned owl's wing
there would be no more than this.

Except the spruce at yard's edge,
snow-brindled, burned brighter blue.
Was there some word you had said,
unnoticed, slipped at the window's

slickness of that tongue of light
on the snow? I saw the whole
of us there, from zero's heights
fallen, in the field's fury swirled.

Nothing in the world seemed good.
Owl killed. Or snake. Fox bled.
But each one from the blue wood
of spruce went forth renewed.

X.

The blue deer walks out on the bridge
of the earth, on tip-ends of grass,
on the dream smoothed cloud of snow.

Fully seen, she makes seasons change
with each slight move of her wingbones.
Her ankles are forever bracelet-bright,

aswirl like planets, and the far center
of the ocean ripples with them. Here,
those who know her know love's flare.

Sorrow mends. Broken toys repair. One
after another, many from either flank
of her ribcage leap out, standing.

New deer, after a while, begin to graze.
Others paw sparks from the sudden ice.
Already drawn apart from these, gravely

gone like pungent smoke into blue air,
this source has been summoned, and is
shadowing another's frank, gazing dream.

Behind her, feeling what black night is,
I write out and say the words we have.
I hope just one will lift its head,

believing its power, remembering the right
incontrovertible sounds of longing
all blue deer are here to answer.

FROM **IN THE HOUSE
OF THE JUDGE**
(1983)

Photographic Plate, Partly Spidered, Hampton Roads, Virginia, with Model T Ford Mid-Channel

No one alive has seen such ice but the five-mile floor
of water so clenched itself salt broke down.
Among us even the age-wearied would not dream
you might walk the Chesapeake Bay
and look unafraid on its lucid darkness,

and the fathers of fathers, boatwrights, sailors of all
waters, never guessed this stuttering machine
might take them so far. But someone,
joking maybe, rolled that small house
on perilous wheels down the banks
of the James, gunned it forward
for skids, runs, circles, a day
of such joyous noise the dead
seemed to have risen, so many
great-booted and black-coated are out there.

We cannot tell what they think, who find themselves
dancing on the road where no road ever was,
out there with the long skirts, a few
thick-waisted grandmothers, even
a scatter of children cast about.
All of them face east to Norfolk
where ships doze like the unimaginable
beasts the sea has given to men's dreams.

The Model T is small, black, plain, and appears
cornered like something risen through ice.
Hands reach in the hazed air
but do not touch what must be
chugging in a kind of terror.
The plate is dotted far and near.
Seagulls? Stains? Some mistake of glass?
Why do their faces look down, as if averted?

Among these is the one who will breed us, having crossed
a whiteness he will not speak about even to her
whose skirts he will shake us from.

114

But now gears spin inside him,
wheels, a future of machines. One day
he will tell my father he walked on water...
sick, chugging for breath, shunned as crazy,
who I remember by the habitual odor of gasoline.
When he died my father said he was too frightened to live.

Under the ice where they walk the dark is enormous.
All day I watch the backs turned away
for the one face that is mine,
that is going to wheel at me the secrets of many.

Of Oystermen, Workboats

The wide, white, wing-boned washboards of twenty
footers, sloped, ridged to hold
a man's tongs and stride,
                          the good stance
to scrape deep with a motion like big applause,
plunging the teeth true beyond the known
mounds of the dead, the current carried
cloisters of murk,
                    miracles that bloom
luminous and unseen, sweet things to be
brought up, bejeweled, culled from husks,

as oystermen like odd angels glide far off enough
to keep a wake gentle as shirts on a line,
red baseball caps dipping like bloodied
heads upright, the clawed hands slapped
at the air in salute,
                       those washboards that splinter
the sun on tongs downlaid, on tines humming,

those womb-hulls harbored flank to flank at dusk
until the white-robed priest of the moon
stands tall to the sea's spume-pour
in nostrils
              of the men who sway from heel to heel,

the season come again, the socketed gray
of their eyes rolling outward,
forearms naked past longjohns,
the salted breast-beaters at first light

lined up, ready to fly.

Smithfield Ham

Aged, bittersweet, in salt crusted, the pink meat
lined with the sun's flare, fissured,
I see far back the flesh fall
as the honed knife goes
through the plate, the lost
voice saying '...it cuts easy as butter...'

Brown sugar and grease tries to hold itself
still beneath the sawed knee's white.
Around the table the clatter of china
kept in the highboy echoes,
children squeal in a near room.

The hand sawing is grandfather's, knuckled,
steadily starting each naked plate
heaped when it ends. Mine
waits shyly to receive
under the tall ceiling
all the aunts, uncle have gathered to hold.

My shirt white as the creased linen, I shine
before the wedge of cherry pie, coffee
black as the sugarless future.

116

My mother, proud in his glance,
whispers he has called for me and for ham.

Tonight I come back to eat in that house the sliced
muscle that fills me with an old thirst.
With each swallow, unslaked, I feel
his hand fall more upon mine,
that odd endless blessing
I cannot say the name of...
it comes again with her family tale,
the dead recalled, the jobless
with low sobs, sickness, the Depression.

Chewing, I ask how he is. Close your mouth, she says.
This time, if he saw me, maybe he'd remember
himself, who thanklessly carved us
the cured meat. The Home holds
him in darkness like coffee
we poured those days. I gnaw
a roll left too long, dried hard.
When my knife drags across the plate,
my mother shakes her head, whining like a child.

Nothing's sharp anymore, I can't help it, she says.
Almost alone, I lift the scalded coffee
steeped black and bitter.
My mouth, as if incontinent,
dribbles and surprises us.
Her face is streaked with summer
dusk where katydids drill and die out.

Wanting to tell her there's always tomorrow,
I say 'You're sunburned. Beautiful as ever.'
Gardening puts the smell of dirt on her.
Like a blade, her hand touches mine.
'More?' Then, 'You'll never get
enough, you think, so sweet,
until the swelling starts,
the ache, the thirst that wants
to bust a person open late at night.'
I fill my cup again, drink, nod, and listen.

Boat Building at Midnight

Wind high in the spruce, like a keel's hiss, leaning
around this stillness, the builder has gone far
in his head, skidding beyond the least
light's outwhirl except the glow he hangs in,

breath spilling away the midges of wood to leave him
in the surf of the *sweep, sweep* his hands make
for the hull of the uncreated to ferry him,
forger of all here, farther than he has ever been.

Already the rib planks sawed rawly are lying pale,
slightly pelvic, and that is not sap seeping
but the salted beads of sweat sprayed down
from his dream's swaying forehead. The hand,

long scarred, uncramps with each stroke of the plane,
faithfully coming, coming, the lathe of breath
from hidden grain lifting a path that loops
uphill above a shore he has never once stepped.

Gusts test his roof and these quicken his making.
His boots slowly fill with the hero's gold
dust he stands over, furring his body
thick as a warrior's beside the first tree honed.

Around him all edges soften, lushly dusted, and he
sees the ridged faces of sleepers, as if dead,
pared smooth as wood in his hands. He hears
the green shroud of spruce leap against the spine

of his moon-silvered roof, feels it, smells the earth
the wind sends. He bears on, blistering himself,
splitting his skin to its first pink, an idea
spread out through his nerves like a flick of fish

up through the net of stars. Holding the wood hard,
seeking the seed-shape of the thing, formed
by what he is forming, he begins to sing
as the young do, heartlessly, and without words

exactly, and quick the dust as salt at his lips.
The blue, flickering workshop light bathes him,
splashes over the yard's spruce root and limb,
pools fathomless, and at stoops of houses laps.

Drudge Crabber

From the workboat plowing
all day the shallow bar
there is lunar white
and nightwoven grass
and the wake's boil
of the crab cage.
It harrows and tosses
the seed, the ghost jelly.
One line, outflown, taut,
controls everything.
When he hauls, his teeth
break bright in the sun.
The cull board gathers.
There is green gone livid
now, flesh loops dancing,
and the chittering crabs
on their white bellies
locked arm in arm.
How does he choose
among all that huddled,
whose hands pitilessly
scrape away the unwanted?
After each of his heapings,
the ring of outriding chain
echoes his ancient wish.
Ocean and planet obey him.
He has always done this.

Snapshot of a Crab-Picker, Among Barrels Spilling Over, Apparently at the End of Her Shift

Clacking and gouging when huddled,
these well-armed warriors
sweat in dimmed sun and scuttle
in the small space each has.
Long arms salute liegelords just
passed, shadows, the honed meat
hard under those scarred helmets.
Sea-promised they come and wait,
season and season always the same.

Near these the squat houses, lights
burled, where a girl will go step
athwart the sharp road of shells
down to a shadow who's dug in
his feathery heels and hovers now
as the liquid night swells, lifts
her with first mooncrest to ride
upon him until she will lie
pale in the frost's breath, spent
flesh the white flaky treasure
these homebound, wordless, breed.

What they offer she will offer,
with sea-smell on her hands
that clean and cradle and keep
against the dull day hours
of simple dreams: hunger, flight,
the tidal force like despair
that under moons shall idle,
singing for the armorless one
love she smiles at, a taste,
faint, she cannot flee ever,
of legions around her biting.

Sister Celia

I went home from my war, walked April's old life, mostly
shunned by my youth's stiffened friends. In truth,
they disbelieved who I was, a fool come seeking
for Speers, Russell, redheaded Celia. What happened?
Them, the lost? Dreamers? Dead. Or else gone to Florida.

Florida! Land of divorce, of the aging child's illusions,
hope, gold skeins of skin, nothing but an idler's
shameless delight. You know how it is, friend: unless
it's trouble you want, a dose you won't ever shake,
sink roots, build a house, pay taxes, thrive. Good

advice. Maybe you'll take it. I did, but that was before
I came here to lie hunched like a snow-buried wren
wanting to shake it all off. They said *misfits, ex-
cheerleaders, bums, crips, fools. Florida, alright!*
Why do we think the past loves us and wants us to call?

I drank, I went where, with Celia, I'd cracked up my car.
I could feel under the tall pines how she'd eased
on me and night started tumbling until we had to
wake up in blood, the world howled with cruisers –
and, Christ, I was GI, ex, busted, singing a bad tune.

Maybe you too think of someone as snow shivers your walls,
but her face won't come, quite, but the rest does, and
only an angel could sigh like she did *Baby, let's go
to Florida.* On my bed of needles I lay, then, thinking
what if she's not gone, not dead, is near? I rose, went

along a lane where cherry blew bright pink. Finding her
house locked, no soul in sight, I circled. I felt
almost freed by the salt-slit river. Then I heard her.
Through echoes of years I descended in shade, it was
my name come whistling out of the green, and her crying

Jesus, look what the cat dragged in! Why you're alive!
That ghostface drew me down into the barn and held me
by an untamed horse and, friend, I lie under this roof
between snow-spit and the iced spruce and I can't
tell you what home is except joy like that, or time

that turns it to shit and leaves you longing to be dead.
Maybe we are only these rotten words, but her song
blew sweet enough to lift me on a stallion named Love,
big and red as a Daytona dusk, a son of a bitch who
heaved me off, who meant worse. Listen, she whacked him

with a fist-thick limb and got me back on, cupping her
hands so I slid in easy, like a cat near a sparrow,
dug heels hard, grappled with hair, and soon roared
straight up. But what goes up, friend, must come
down, so I did, in the softest, greenest shit. All smiles.

Should I have cried Lord, what else can you do to me?
A man always thinks there's nothing more. Ache is.
It waits malignant, naked, the worm in love's words.
If you should wake in blackness, cracked, not dead,
certain the one you hold is, you might see what I mean.

You don't have to dream of all you've done, wreckage,
or gags on a sweet yellow face in a Saigon alley.
Just lie still. It's easy to feel the silk sheets
where the moon swells high over Daytona, the radio's
blues bristling long distance. Listen for bracelets

as she lifts the phone, red hair bucked loose, the ocean
of stars lapping her patio. Well, easy to feel
if your head's as lonely as each night flushing out
years like her smell. Do you think she might call yet?
Maybe in April, when the yard needs you, and the kids.

Here it comes, the ringing starts, the lifesaver's voice
says *Why, you're alive!* There's nothing worse, God
knows, to drag you from room to room like a mouse
the cat loves, those words pounding – oh Christ,
phone ring, sing, buckle through the blackness baby, for

isn't it Celia calling you home, calling through the ice,
her voice hot as blood in her face? Listen, what
do you want, friend, but life's little bell zinging,
calling collect, saying please come home, *Baby?*
Fool, before it's too late answer. Say yes. You'll pay.

Bats

Still in sleeping bags, the promised delivery
only words as usual, our lives upside down,
we are transients lost in thirteen rooms
built by a judge who died. The landlord says
they mean no harm, the bats, and still I wake
at the shrill whistling, the flutter overhead.

I fumble to a tall window open among maples.
A car crawling a hill splashes my face with light
spread fine by mist that had been summer rain,
a sweetness that drips from black-palmed leaves.
The breeze I feel is fresh, edged with mown hay,

enough to make me think the thumps and titters
I hear might be the loving pleasure of parents
unguessed, a long quarrel ended, a thrilling
touch that trails to muffled play. But these
are bats, shadows, residents of the house elders
built to last, the vaulted attic tall as a man

holding them hung in rows daylong like words
unuttered above the yard where children romp.
Flashlight in hand, I pass through the parlor
papered in silk for marriages the judge made,
and stand beneath the hidden door. The truth is

nothing can drive them out or contravene those
fretful, homespinning voices we cannot help
fearing as if they were the all-knowing dead.
Yet if I had one chair to stand tall enough on
I would climb with my light and shaking voice
to see whatever has lodged in their glittery eyes.

Under a room I have never seen but know, I stand
like one of the unblessed at the edge of dawn.
Smelling mold, I hear a dog's hopeless howl
and think of the stillness in the waking heads
of those who hang in sleep: it may be like love

in the children we cannot keep unharmed for long.
Each one near me is furled in a homeholding song no
darkness or deed can kill. With them all dreams
bring the fields' fresh life here to hum over.
As if I had never been out of this place, I listen.
The sound is like rain, leaves, or sheets settling.

Turn-of-the-Century House

The leaded, wiggly glass lives in its human length
as the squall, unpredicted, slams me down late
at night to see what in the world goes on wailing.
We have no lights. Lightning like a girl's grin
stands me dead center of the parlor. It's maples.

This house has its jitters yet. It's unreconstructed,
two claw-footed bathtubs, taps that won't turn off,
doors refusing their frames. Often they danced here.
Stars on the tin roof marked the place from near hills,

settling thick as a shawl on a woman shaken awake.
It was only memory, but she woke her sisters anyway.
They stood on linoleum. Glass rattled and pipes clanged.
A bad storm, couldn't they see that? Ice, then snow.

The maples no one could bear cutting down, dangerous now,
raked the roof. Stars turned to ice, blinding the glass.
Can you see them, trying to sing as you would? Cold
swirls at the feet, dull yellow, naked as planked maple.
Water in the pipes forms red-streaked and pearl nails.

House Movers

Steadily down highways intractable roofs creep.
Whoever chooses them seems of one mind.
Sad white, pale green, the imagined result
of a going-out-of-business operation,
their clapboard hulls betray storied weather
by flaking paint and those stone-cracked
glasses just violated. Behind them steps
hang patiently, or a family porch waits
like a quick amazed countryman. Required,
we think, are brute shoulders, blue jaws
and knuckles that gently graze a child's
face sliding under the edge of sleep.
These do not go with the houses, moored
families who seem alive only near pastures
where their fathers have lain for years.
Empty of each worn table and broken chair
used long nights to conjure, talk, puzzle,
the houses glide over our roads like veins,
ominous as we pass them and grip our wheels.
Wherever they arrive hard ground is gouged,
papers solemnly signed, lime is laid out,
the gray, bony bite of foundations readied.
We imagine, driving sometimes behind them,
the black birdwings will start up, spiral,
a furred knob in the sumac will shudder,
clench itself down, and growl in its belly.
In a week no one will stop to feel suddenness
hunch unalterably there, like a growth,
or months after will remember what was
never so stingingly white. But shouldered
quietly at that rutted ground, our children
those first hours wait for children to pop out.
They lick their lips at the future come
as unlikely as death or birth among them.
Here, too, arrive the unsummoned about us,
from the tree-shrouded edges we live near,
the thick-thighed ones who pull and strike,
wielders of maul and nail and cold chain.
When we step in their tracks we become

the bare-soled children of their keeping.
We dance out of their way, transfixed.
At night, our houses locked, we cannot guess
who chose how we would lie under all this.
In our heads their walls ring, bow, and chant.

Your Christmas Present

This year we are sending you combs of honey
from Jaynes Farm, only six hard miles
west of the village where we live.
I have run with my body that far.
All summer I approached the apple trees
burning their best green light that
has now turned gold. We wish you
the green-gone-to-gold running of joy.
We wish you to remember the nights
long and black heaving star glitter
in the bees who ran on the hours of air,
giving the gift of themselves in gold.
We have wrapped this in local spruce
that it may smell clean and stay good.
We believe the wind sings us together.
Tonight our family is standing in the yard,
under the godly blue spruce, wearing
the magical light of the star mantel.
A long window light keeps our feet gold.
If you were here you would stand with us
to face Jaynes Farm where the bees wait
to work and the apple trees shiver again
and deer crane their necks upward, ghosts
who cross and recross the human road.
On your breads, when you come to eat,
squeeze the comb between your hands
so the gold runs out and gleams. Do not
consume the white husk or the green limbs,
else you may feel the coming of hooves
and the odd fanning of wings behind you.

Beyond this we have to advise everyone
there are gaping holes and you must
squeeze hard to think of us, filling them.

Snow Owl

In snow veined with his blood, the white bruise
of a broken wing, the hiss of his mouth
salute my hand. What dark mouth
has torn his pink flesh so?
Big as I am he would nail me
with those nubs never made to walk,
wings trusted like a prayer all his nights. *Here*

Here, I cluck, on my knees edging toward him,
my own belief the cunning of words.
His eye cocks, the hinged horn
of the beak tracks and rasps,
gathers its voice, shrills,
shrieks with a wind's rage.
This is the only language given his kind.

I cast my call around him, soft syllables
like an ice he will never escape.
At each angle his bad wing
gusts a storm of snow
between us, a blind faith.
Sometimes I leave him, beaten,
who I cannot abandon in this life

today gone new-flecked by blood, by snow's
feathering moonwhite. I watch him lift
in his will, fall back to blackness,
to time and ice – his eye cocked
with unsayable secrets
beating onward, blinking.
Around us small towns huddle, lights on.

In the House of the Judge

All of them asleep, the suspiring everywhere is audible weight
   in the winter-shadowed house where I have dreamed
      night after night and stand now trying
  to believe it is only dust, no more than vent-spew
     risen from the idiotically huffing
grandfather of a furnace in the coal room's heart of darkness.

Haven't I touched the flesh-gray sift on bookshelves, on framed
   dim photographs of ancestors, on the clotted arms
      of the banjo clock that tolls past
  all resemblance to time and clicks like a musket's
steel hammer? And every day I wipe my glasses but still it comes,
   as now, at the top of the whining stairs, I am

come to wait with my hand laid light on the moon-slicked railing.
   I hear the house-heave of sleepers, and go jittery
      with no fear I can name. I feel myself
    shaped by the mica-fine motes that once were one
     body in earth until gouged, cracked,
left tumbled apart and scarcely glowing in a draft-fanned pit.

Pipes clank and gargle like years in the ashen veins of the Judge
   when they came to his house, the dung-heeled, some
      drunk, all with stuttered pleas to free
  their young, who could make it given a chance, just
one more good chance, so they said. Impassive, in skin-folds thick
    as a lizard, he stared at the great one for a sign,

the dog across the room, who kept wary eye and was a one-man dog.
   Overhead do the same unbearable stars yet wheel
     in bright, ubiquitous malice, and what
    am I, wiping my glasses, certain this house walks
     in nail-clicking threat, going to plead?
I look out through warped Civil War glass buffed by men now ash

where the small park he gave in civic pride lies snow-blistered.
   Subzero then, as now, sent fire in the opening
      throat, but they came: tethered horses,
    striding shadows, and women who shrieked nightlong
until even gone they continued in his head. He heard them breathe.
   He painted his house perfectly white.

I stare at that snow as at a scaffold. Whose lightening footprints
could soften my fear or say why I sniff like a
dog, seem to taste a skim of black air
upsweeping the maple stairwell, and feel my hair
go slowly white? How many hours must
a man watch snow shift the world before he sees it is only a dream

of useless hope stamped and restamped by the ash-steps of those we
can do no justice to except in loving them? But
what could he do before the raw facts
of men cleaving flesh like boys hacking ice?
I think how he must have thought of his barking teacher of law:
There is only truth and law! He had learned the law.

But what was the truth to leave him trembling, a child in prayer?
In late years he kept the monster by his side, two shades
walking alone in the ice, the nail-raker, one
who howled without reason and clawed at the heart
of door after door. In the end he was known
inseparable from his beast who, it was said, kept the Judge alive.

Until he was not. Until his house emptied. Until we came who I hear
breathing, those heads warm as banked ash under my hand
laid light as I have laid it on this railing.
But are we only the upfloating and self-clinging ash
that loops freely through dark houses? Those enigmatic fissures
I see circling the snow – are those only the tracks

of the dog I locked out, those black steps no more than a gleaming
ice, or the face of some brother in the dirt betrayed,
pleading, accusing? The moon, far off and dim,
plays tricks with my eyes and the snow path turns dark as
a line of men marched into the earth. Whitely, my breath floats
back at me, crying *I did not do this*, when the shuddering

courthouse clock past the green booms me back to myself. Dream's
aftershock, the heirloom banjo starts to thud and drum
so I turn and hustle downstairs to halt it.
Even with my hands laid on its hands it wants to thump
its malicious heart out, but I can do this
at least: I can hold on to help them sleep through another night.

I can sit for a time with love's ice-flickering darkness where ash
is heavily filling my house. I can sit with my own
nailed walker in the snow, one whistled
under my hand without question or answer. If I sleep
he will pad the floors above the fire-pit. He will claw me awake
to hear breathing in the still house of the Judge

where I live.

FROM **GRAY SOLDIERS**

(1983)

Night Traffic Near Winchester, Virginia

From Cumberland's funerals, eldest son, I
lead my survivors south, toward the sea,
past tall ash, through stunning cidery
winesaps still bobbing the Blue Ridge,
the leaf-littered fieldstone walls
drooping like rebel stragglers away
from weathered barns, veterans solemn,
quaint as postcards from the dark
Tomb of the Confederate Dead, never
closed, catching the trucks' roar
at Winchester where my father always
stopped to rest. Here, we descend

into the Valley, slow to a stop-and-go
crawl through painted brick cottages
huddled at sidewalks like history,
heartpine floors sloped so badly
water runs off before it stains.
Like the hips of ancestors, each
foundation is cracked and patched,
the windows narrow as eyes, crusty
along the once horse-clotted street.
Tourists find here the cheery, yellow
farmhouse used by Stonewall Jackson
to plot cavalry raids thunderous
as the black Bible he slept with.
It's dark as a mapcase now, unread.

I promise kids we'll stop another time,
long enough to see boots, old orders,
the grim portraits staring at war,
but now we climb, car straining, up
the last northern ridge, and halt
before our drop to the plains. Here
my father stopped with me, heading
north to bury fallen kin. Stepping
out, the chill, rare night drifts
me back to the smell of his coffee.

This is the way to your grandmother's,
he'd say, pointing at sky, so I say it,
on the cliff, no grandmother left.
Behind us nothing's changed, motors
howl all night, voices that roar
as teamsters did, hearing the rumor –
'Grant's taken Charlottesville,'
but tonight just the march of boys
looking for girls, trucks for home.
It's only Route 17, the country way.

But my son, old as I was with my father,
climbs over our sleeping girls, steps
to the overlook's lipfall I don't
need to look at, historical dark
that never stops falling here. Still,
I come behind him, take his hand.
His athletic jacket shines like cities
at Christmas, its faint galaxies
of light shifting as the body moves.
Out there we see the neon welcome
of blue Sears, red K-Mart, streets
steady with taillights like campfires.

When once I asked my father why armies
fought here those long nights, he said
We were boys just going up and down.
Afraid, homeless, glad for a fire.
Our fathers and fathers of fathers.
In the cold of mountains I'm afraid
at this edge and feel the hand asking
'How far have we come?' I could say
I don't know, the usual evasion,
but over the lights, the dotted road,
I hear an old voice I had thought lost
say *Far, but not far enough yet.*
Ahead, our family will stand awake,
lights on, coffee hot, ready for news.

Bullet Tree: Camden, North Carolina

The most fearful and best contested struggle of the Burnside Expedition
OFFICIAL RECORDS UNION & CONFEDERATE ARMIES

A steeped murmur works through young pines,
    slowly the shadows shimmer apart,
  wind, and something worse than wind comes
to draw me close, a tourist where family fought.

One trunk's bark-wounds seep black sap, splitting
    time's scab long utterly hard, lead
  like guilts deeply embedded, unfreed, still
perfectly pure in this wood's tallest father.

Dwarfed by our swollen ancestor, its limbs
    weather-warped, fragile, so, cut,
  planed, the engendered must be blemished
by dark whorls secret as rot. Each bushing

scrub tightens on this story, grows repeating it,
    until even roots and frail saplings
  distant from the crown as grandsons know
the scar's mark like nerve failure, or disease.

One tree climbed by children in Camden is
    standing yet, gray, gnarled, leaking.
  The plaque says 'last of its kind'. Never
to be cut down or nailed. Graffiti says 'Why?'

Photograph of a Confederate Soldier Standing on Rocks in the James River at Richmond

                   A light rises,
falls, floats around the frame, a kind
of water swirling through generations
of years, pooling and shining when we look

at oblique corners, a given-back glimmer of one
come from a thatch of hickory heaving the home-field
still in his head, this boy turned in the sun's
stunned spilling where the river is
bristly as bayonets rippling,
                                        one hung in light
like a leaf above that lipping darkness,
the hem of his greatcoat outflung.

                    Why is he there? What man
in the war's middle stands like this with the teeth-
ragged remains of Richmond looming to the north?
We think he may dream of days the acorns
shelled down through yellow leafburst,
or mother's hand on him because in pools
the brackish bluegills would not
let him go home on time. Why
do we not think of a throat's thick fear?
Can fear be that shining on his face? Maybe

                    Fall's glory
that must be in each thread of the sorry homespun
he has taken through a toil of sun somehow
lets loose, leaves him alone. All his life
he remembers this walk, this stone-cradle turning
his face up to cliffs. We can almost see him think
not once can he say why he came, nor give any answer
for what in this split second nails him forever
as no bullet could.
                    Expressionless, he seeks us,
one-eyed, an eyepatch rampant over the left shoulder,
the right eye dark as a wound, and he cannot see
all the light in the world holds us to him,
all we are, the uncreated future,
                              the image
which begins here as one apprehension
in the nerves of men, the secret
bond we almost know in that
instant we turn and lift ourselves
from the black river-roar and light-swarm.

Ironclad

I'm ten, spending the summer with my grandmother,
let loose, wandering the mossed bulkhead
where the tide swings too far in
to walk the little sand of Hampton Roads.

I sit in the grass under the steel historical sign
that says if I look a hundred blue years out
I'll see that battle of the first Ironclads,
three hours of clanging and no decision,

no casualties until at noon the Monitor's cheesebox
hull shudders, its sight hole flares wide,
blinding the skipper, Lieutenant Worden.
I think of those seamen, speechless in chugging blue

where a peach in my hand is soft as a skull, one side
going red with the dusk while the Purple Martins
swoop, sleek shadows, so close I hear
the wingbeats like distant hearts. But I don't

eat, I don't move when my name steams out of the dark.
How can I when I haven't seen the battle end,
those iron tubs fighting like twins, night
already pushing them back in the wind? Off Hatteras

one day I'll see a squad of divers cast nets of light
over sand holding the Monitor like a woman asleep.
What brings the storm, moves the ship, hides
still its crew's heartbeat in cold blue

tons of water until radar finds it again clear
as a tumor on florescent screens? None of us knows
how to resurrect this ghost. Electric pings
report odd calling sounds, maybe weather, but

turned blue and gray by the tv's newscast
on this Atlantic night, I hear my grandmother
promise to find me in storms. She did. Her face
feathers near, calls past pumping machines, then

sinks as the hospital, iron engines beat on.
I was ten, watching squadrons of killdeer.
Oh sailors of the dark, I want your whistle
to haul me aboard. I want to hear you call forever.

A Nest of Mice

The blackened, dew-wet fingers of the glove
I found to wear that morning
in my grandmother's potato bin give

again the chill I felt as I lifted that brood
from her cellar one late day in March.
Five blind thumbs. I heard Hampton Roads,

its marsh tips stroked by the wind, its wail
and hiss like sails over docks long
rotting where slaves stood once for sale.

I listened. I did as I had been told.
Gasoline is quick, it severs
the life purely, it gathers up the gold

of flesh consumed. Today in my garden parched
by drought, I weed with those hands.
Fierceness of fire will scour out the worst,

they said, but I find the tracks in the rows.
The duskfalls of Spring skitter back
like the dead. I think of her tall window

where first sun would burn through my sleep.
In weeds wind sniffed like a dog.
In the cellar we piled the apples to keep

while we hacked the earth into the furrows
for seeds, and for gleaners of seeds.
Yet all are now dead and lie under crows

black as what seeps out where fire sizzles.
I feel myself watched in the sun.
Under my knees I sense those who sit still

near our blustery, ancestral house. I'm pouring
gas clear as water, my head sweaty.
Then it's dark. I'm waiting. The floor squeaks.

I have gone to bed dirty, scorched, and won't wash.
They say I'm too little, but I'll live.
Their light flickers close. I hear them hush.

Seven Pines: Taking Shelter from the Rain

Deer Shoot: I

I'm east of Richmond in my car. Bugs ping
my windshield where once pine rose, a slate blue
day when we first walked this killing ground, things
jumping at our feet so fast we'd load, shoot

you said, as if we'd hit the battle's heart,
no side ours. That brassy swath of broomstraw
like a bed where the creek oozed was our start.
Doves cooed from phone wires – remember? Cold raw,

but shifting in bitter winds, rain in spits.
I shivered. You killed an old crow, a loon.
You'd blast whatever showed, like manic vets
hardened past rules. There was a faint boom-boom

downstream, too strong for even a ten-gauge.
We were spooked as we settled in for deer,
as if some cannon's century-old rage
coiled back. I jumped each time you bellowed *Here,*

you bastards! – blasting skies with both barrels,
surprising no bored Yankees. A bad joke,
the way we hunted. When, panicked, I whirled
and killed a spruce, I missed the only buck

we'd see that sorry year we slipped past gray
stone walls, two boys lost at home. But blue fled,
and late, in sleet drizzle, we hunched our way
back like survivors, beaten, no word when

we'd hunt again, glad to be out, to leave
the gutted dead to rot on vines like wire.
Is it hatred of ourselves or dull peace
makes us violent without need, fathers

long gone, their harms nothing we have to fear?
But, Virginians, we're double-bound: we boast
we'd fight in their place. So we kill their deer.
Can't we see what veterans' faces show?

Those eyes, hard, black, blank as a loon's in rot.
They shine where I drive, leaping from the road.
That boom-boom? Developers. Parking lots
for Sears, boutiques, *Battlefield Mall*. In gold.

Days, nights they pour in, smug crowds, confident
new malls keep the country right. Evil's out.
The dead are dishonored here. We choose what
we want buried. With cash. I want to shout

at baldy in his flag-flogged truck, *Fuck you!*
Like a copter over jungle, I aim
my nose past your home. Snipers, see, will shoot
boys like us in the hat. Let's hunt. It rains.

Rabbits: II

December, hunting rabbits,
we heard the big guns
hidden far in the sumac.
Boys at it since dawn,

another ice blue went gray.
We walked over the creek
where the dogs bayed.
Nothing yet but our luck

would change. We'd raise
three in a short hour.
Your shotgun pasted
each to soy beans. More

as the afternoon drained
to blue-black and broke
finally to hard rain.
Plodding, we had no hope

but found a shack, grave
with age, the rusty roof
leaking like a sieve.
Harder sleet pinged off

the tin like anger's shrapnel.
It grew colder between us.
Ice, then, on home roads fell
slick and murderous.

I said *Let's go*. You wouldn't.
Like the fathers, trapped,
we'd coil ourselves, slip
heat man to man. But that

couldn't keep killing cold off.
We rubbed hands, breathed steam,
as you said the dead taught.
Fear is the shivering dream

I have of that ghost place
vanished in *Battlefield Mall*.
There's not a single face
except Death's I could call,

the one I see blindly running,
upended in ankle-breaking muck.
Face down, you're screaming
in the memory cracked

because I still carry you,
and your letters from Vietnam.
You wrote *Screw the gooks,*
screw our fathers, screw home,

screw liars and lovers of war!
Your photo looked like habit:
fatigues, M-16, the whore.
Mine answered, a string of rabbits.

Gray Soldiers: III

What is it Yeats says, nothing whole until rent?
I want each day now to be that.
I want to chatter and drink until we've spent
all the gray in us, all the lies.

Steady rain falls on the patio, on the steel
muzzle of the James River, its plink, plink
through pines almost a roof, or walls
risen again to shelter us. I want you

to shoulder through those frail planks, to rise
from mud like those ancestors we failed,
the dead at our backs we called pride.
Once we hoped we'd live purely to kill.

Spring climbs to canopy the woods with green
you'd call heroic. I'd once have said
mindless. Now dogwood bursts and careens
like fat coveys against hacked trunks.

Today my chimney admits a wash of rain, drop
after drop feathering the ashpit. Young,
we marched up and down with dead kin, troops
of righteous warriors, our monitor ghosts.

This late I want to say nothing matters anymore.
When I do the wind's wet shirt slaps at
the black glass I watch. It isn't over,
my chill seems to claim, meaning loss –

but also the answering world of consequence.
This morning down the hill I saw cardinals,
bluejays, and off the James three egrets
whose flight burned the air like sunrise.

Was this absolution? For what? And crows then,
clattering like old hatred. But not. Crows
only, in hunger. Unarmed, I drew them
in pantomime sights as you would, and pulled.

Was it I meant to kill something in myself?
Your wounded hat sat loose on my head.
What if men could kill killing itself?
Coming home I found seven sapling pines

and thought them an omen, so sprawled on my back.
Like Whitman, in my own truce, I remembered
you leaving for Da Nang, the plane's track
runic in snow. Before that, the door

in the fuselage wall, you in uniform shouting
what we thought was *Do good, hunt for me.*
I wondered where, and with what? Things
heal and end, except the wounds of words.

Hunt for me. Was this what Christ the soldier said?
And each father to new boys, their sons
open-faced for love, who die to understand
why the seasons break them apart? What's meant?

Boys hunt to live, grunting words, whacking sticks.
You died to save a mall for kids to roam.
You came back stiff. Water in the creek
that day sprang like struck guitar string.

It's not much, this life we have, but no wars today.
Under the pines I sprawled down in a cat came
with a sparrow half-alive, half-flayed,
toyed-with like me, like you,

framed by the world indifferent to hunter and hunted.
Thinking about us, I followed the cat home.
Egrets were in my mind. And rusted guns.
Spring silked blue. Things had started to bloom.

142

Leafless Trees, Chickahominy Swamp

Humorless, hundreds of trunks, gray in the blue expanse
where dusk leaves them hacked like a breastwork,
stripped like pikes planted to impale, the knots
of vines at each groin appearing placed by makers
schooled in grotesque campaigns. Mathew Brady's
plates show them as they are, the ageless stumps,
timed-sanded solitaries, some clumped in squads
we might imagine veterans, except they're only wood,
and nothing in the world seems more dead than these.

Stopped by the lanes filled with homebound taillights,
we haven't seen the rumored Eagle we hoped to watch,
only a clutch of buzzards ferrying sticks for a nest.
Is this history, that we want the unchanged, useless
spines out there to thrust in our faces the human
qualities we covet? We read this place like generals
whose promised recruits don't show, who can't press on:
we feel the languor of battle, troops unable to tell
themselves from the enemy, and a file-hard fear gone

indifferent in the mortaring sun that will leave all
night after night standing in the same cold planes
of water. It never blooms or greens. It merely stinks.
Why can't we admit this is death's gift, the scummy
scene of our pride, blown brainpans of a century ago?
Who do we sit and sniff the rank hours inside words
blunt as ground that only stares off our question: what
happened? Leaf-light in our heads, don't we mean why
these grisly emblems, the slime that won't swell to hope?

The rapacious odor of swamps all over the earth bubbles
sometimes to mist, fetid flesh we can't see but know
to be cells composing, decomposing, a heart's illusions.
God knows what we'd do in there, we say, easing back
on the blacktop. Once we heard a whistling. Harmonicas?
But who'd listen? Surely all was green once, fragile
as a truce, words braiding sun and water, as on a lake
where families sang. What else would we hope for, do
in the dead miles nothing explains or changes or relieves?

Caravati's Salvage: Richmond, Virginia

He's the reaper, the buyer, the keeper of grand houses
gone to pieces, and the choice parts are here.
You want big doors, brass knobs, stained glass?
A hand-carved bed? Grandfather clocks? A chandelier?

Maybe those shutters that lined Monument Avenue,
heartwood pine, paint age-blistered, kept closed
a decade, by war widows, when Lee died? Or you
desire staircase railing, marble mantels, bellows –

he's stacked it all in heaps high as a pile of guns.
Ask. Caravati keeps. Endless old names, how they lived.
Eighty-three, hair white as nightgowns in the sun,
he'll guide you, touching each piece, a man you'd give

your heart to, in his foyer, summoned by his bell,
with secrets we covet. When you come, he delights.
He offers water, a beaded jar, from a hidden well.
The one his fathers dug. Way down, cold, sweet.

Reliable Heat

Delivers from distances of wood, dumptruck squalling,
a nation of red dirt wedged in its seams,
the hoist's screech a child
abandoned under big shirts flapping on a line.

Good mix, my black countryman says, stooped at his rig.
God's plenty of heat in that heavy log.
Feel it, meaning my wife, her
kind always tells, city or country, don't matter.

Stacking steadily, shirt off, brown as a pine, he's
a rooster at work, chattering a country's
need, lateborn mouths that wait.
I imagine the shadows he's cut in their place.

He warns me it's the hardheads hold out the longest,
wedged in like family. A heat to keep the hearth blessed.

144

FROM **THE ROUNDHOUSE VOICES**

(1985)

The Roundhouse Voices

In full glare of sunlight I came here, man-tall but thin
as a pinstripe, and stood outside the rusted fence
with its crown of iron thorns while
the soot cut into our lungs with tiny diamonds.
I walked through houses with my grain-lovely slugger
from Louisville that my uncle bought and stood
in the sun that made its glove soft on my hand
until I saw my chance to crawl under and get past
anyone who would demand a badge and a name.

The guard hollered I could get the hell from there quick
when I popped in his face like a thief. All I ever wanted
to steal was life and you can't get that easy
in the grind of a railyard. *You can't catch me,*
lardass, I can go left or right good as the Mick,
I crooned to him, holding my slugger by the neck
for a bunt laid smooth where the coal cars
jerked and let me pass between tracks
until, in a slide on ash, I fell safe and heard
the wheeze of his words: *Who the hell are you, kid?*

I hear them again tonight, Uncle, hard as big brakeshoes,
when I lean over your face in the box of silk. The years
you spent hobbling from room to room alone crawl
up my legs and turn this house to another
house, round and black as defeat, where slugging
comes easy when you whip the gray softball over
the glass diesel globe. Footsteps thump on the stairs
like that fat ball against bricks and when I miss
I hear you warn me to watch the timing, to keep
my eyes on your hand and forget the fence,

hearing also that other voice that keeps me out and away
from you on a day worth playing good ball. Hearing
Who the hell... I see myself like a burning speck
of cinder come down the hill and through a tunnel
of porches like stands, running on deep ash,
and I give him the finger, whose face still gleams
clear as a B&O headlight, just to make him get up

and chase me into a dream of scoring at your feet.
At Christmas that guard staggered home sobbing,
the thing in his chest tight as a torque wrench.
In the summer I did not have to run and now

who is the one who dreams of a drink as he leans over
tools you kept bright as a first girl's promise? I
have no one to run from or to, nobody to give
my finger to as I steal his peace. Uncle, the light
bleeds on your gray face like the high barbed-wire
shadows I had to get through and maybe you don't remember
you said to come back, to wait and you'd show me
the right way to take a hard pitch in the sun
that shudders on the ready man. I'm here though

this is a day I did not want to see. In the roundhouse
the rasp and heel-click of compressors is still,
soot lies deep in every greasy fingerprint.
I called you from the pits and you did not come up
and I felt the fear when I stood on the tracks
that are like stars which never lead us
into any kind of light and I don't know who'll
tell me now when the guard sticks his blind snoot
between us: take off and beat the bastard out.
Can you hear him over the yard, grabbing his chest,
cry out, *Who the goddamn hell are you, kid?*

I called him every name in the book, Uncle, but he caught us
and what good did all those hours of coaching do?
You lie on your back, eyeless forever, and I think
how once I climbed to the top of a diesel and stared
into that gray roundhouse glass where, in anger,
you threw up the ball and made a star
to swear at greater than the Mick ever dreamed.
It has been years but now I know what followed
every morning the sun came up, not light
but the puffing bad-bellied light of words.

All day I've held your hand, trying to say back a life,
to get under that fence with words I lined
and linked up and steamed into a cold room
where the illusion of hope means skin torn

on tools. The footsteps come pounding into words
and even the finger I give death is words
that won't let us be what we wanted, each one
chasing and being chased by dreams in the dark.
Words are all we ever were and they did us
no damn good. Do you hear that?

Do you hear the words that, in oiled gravel, you gave me
when you set my feet in the right stance to swing?
They come coal-hard and they come in wings
and loops like despair not even the Mick
could knock out of this room, words softer
than the centers of hearts in guards or uncles,
words skinned and numbed by too many bricks.
I've had enough of them and bring them back here
where the tick and creak of everything dies
in your tiny starlight and I stand down
on my knees to cry *Who the hell are you, kid?*

Remembering Harpers Ferry

White, slope-shouldered, falling away in shade
as the land falls, windows half-shuttered,
odd glass eyes in the cool morning of fogs.

The seam where each wind will howl is clear,
angles of slats still binding, scarred, the strain
of wood that's warped by bitter winters – who

lived here? we ask, slowing, imagining ourselves
in the cupola tilted like old hope. We stop
and trespass the slant of abandoned floors, steps,

furtive as a family in our talk of what's left.
Here the marriages, divorces, deaths of good wood
remain, mute beginnings, quaint in the snapshots

our children will box up in time: a rotten walk
we took, a tumbled foundation, ancestral hills
that keep heaving up wildflowers, planks, seams.

An Antipastoral Memory of One Summer

It is written that a single hurricane holds the power
to run our whole country for one year. Imagine
lights in Minnesota chicken coops, firebells
ringing every borough of New York, dock pumps
spewing the bilge from Louisiana shrimpers,
the pulse that sends a voice from San Francisco
to Nagasaki where a woman wakes, folds, and refolds
the American edition of news already forgotten.

Yet even in the dark silos of our countrymen who
practice graceful moves at the missile's panel
(that is like a piano with the amazing, unplayed
notes not even Beethoven could hear into fusion),
no one dreams how to harness the storm for good.
That is why I think of two people at a bulkhead,
an old woman desperately holding down the hem
of her flowered dress, holding a boy's small hand
where the waves they have come to see blossom

one after another, sluicing over their driven hair,
the salt sting so strong their eyes begin to swell,
until they fall back across the elegant Boulevard,
and even there the unexpected crescendos boom in
laces and strings of water radiant as new light.
The noise is unforgettable and deafening, the sea
keeps orchestrating, as if it means to address
all our preparations, the boarded windows, the dead

cars with their rain-blistered glass, the sidewalk
clotted now with seaweed like abandoned bodies.
That suddenly, then, the calm eye stalls on them,
a stillness like a lock with no key, a hand
hovering at a switch, waiting for music unheard,
and see – the woman turns, drags the boy hard
past oaks older than them both, its leaves this fall
blinking like lights, trembling, limbs like spears,
two entering a powerless house to huddle, to pray
to the still God, though they call it hurricane.

Ear Ache

The Great Depression sat on my grandfather
like Dante's Ugolino eating the malignancy
that betrayed him to insatiable hunger.
Left a lifelong fulminator at destiny,

he knew nothing he made or said would last.
My mother learned how to ignore him, the hatred,
coarse cursing, and door-slamming at chance.
He played big-band trumpet in twenty-eight.

Then the country went bad and his ear broke
when the factories juked back to the banging
work he had to take. Grandmother's stroke,
the family saddled him with misery.

Yet he came one drab, silent night, hunched
over my body coiled in a feverish bed,
growled about self-pity, and reached
to lay his scar-sizzled welder's hand

at flesh that glowed like his Camel cigarette.
The doctors had nodded over me for years –
'Maybe he'll grow out of it – yet it
swelled back each winter, overwhelming cures

with sourceless pus. Penicillin, wonder drugs,
even radium needles shoved up my nose,
nothing worked. I'd lay limp as a rag
under books my mother stacked like hopes

their dulcet voices, calling, could blunt
my will to jam in fingers at the ache.
I still see him bend close, that stunted
avatar of my line, his eyes slag-gray,

his ash piked coronal with deep inhaling.
The smoke he blows in my ear like words
tickles and stinks so I almost feel
his weld's fury, his skin's raw blisters

when darkness opens and he finds me near,
crying that other day. 'You'll go blind,
you little bastard, if you look at the fire.'
But it's in me already, the hammered bond

that rings in my ear, the heat and ache.
The bubbling flux, fire's spit, what's in
his monstrous headgear – I forget. Not the rage,
as he grips me, hurting, forcing this vision

to spiral back now, the crooked stoop of a man,
dirty-nailed, ashen, smoking from the nose.
his lips at my ear, sadness taking my hand
to make the hopeless song he puffs and blows.

The Family

In leaf green and brown vests, these shepherds
                of civility, hunters,
        stand in the sight of cousin and uncle,
echoes of words all that links me to them now
                when the night's sleet

gusts at my window, its shudder that thud of shot-
                guns over distant
        ground. My steaming coffee shows me
flushed from the wood's lip as I break to the cries
                they heave, words

triangulating to locate the home flight of doves
                down in impenetrable
        tangles of thorns and roots. I drop myself
into that stillness like the soul out of the sun,
                scrambling to hide

as the dove did, remembering their lessons, feathers
                of my skin pulled back
        to quick red, then I find it, a blink-
less husk I cradle and bring back in a man's too-big
                bag-coat. For this

I rose into the flesh-blue last light, the last
        time I was a boy
    disarmed and running, nearly one
of those who would stand while the tearing wings
        feathered fingers

with the little glue of blood, that papery ripping
        of breast so faint
    it was almost lost – but it stuck
in my head with the gut smell and weightless dance
        of tufts floating

like the breeze-rifled hair of my father. I
        see palm-sized
    bodies stripped on our kitchen's
counter, hear knives that click, the banging of
        the open breech,

smell the vanilla-sweet Hoppe's oil as I huddle at
        geometry's secrets
    while my father tells me I must try
to know more than the family has. This is the low
        moan of field talk –

guttural, innocent as love, half-understood under
        first seedburst of stars.
    When I brought them doves each would clap
an ungloved hand on my shoulder, breath would dart out
        in wing-rush until I

grew exhausted in this dream of manhood. Sometimes
        I hunched, unmoving,
    hidden in thickets as their pellets spent
through that trunk-world, ticking. They called me
        forth, the killers,

to blackness at field's edge, to feathery flesh-heaps.
        I would be silent,
    the smallest, learning to hear each cry
back 'Night!' as he veered, and went, not knowing
        this wasn't goodbye,

was only the family name for whoever must stand last
            like a heartbeat
        left with its shadow, the father squinting
past numbers and kitchen glare, thermometer plunging
            to zero, one wisp

of feather stuck to the cheek I still kissed goodnight.
            Against black glass
        shining pellets of ice cluster, points
and melting lines urgent as faces hurling me to the ground
            of the abandoned,

and speechless bodies draining in the sink at dawn.
            Dark and nasty
        birds, in my head they are still as
beautiful as theorems, equations I cannot resolve
            to helpless answers.

Drafted

Downtown, in the Federal Building, a temple
of governments and WPA fathers where
once you could see people, fields,
tall plumes of smoke, a river,
we enter and peel ourselves
among white-coated officials.
A shoed line of countrymen,
we take up the position,
hoping only for family
darkness at day's end but
ready to endure what we must.

Each shuffles behind his new brother
through barren rooms whose
utility's unknown. Some
pass without words, gray,
having no hope to see
hillsides they left,

shaken here by numbers.
Others joke, provided
with sealed black marks
from family doctors.
We are equal, they say.

Each spreads fingers to cover
his secret, some clean
some filth-crusted, heads
kept mostly down, as if
spilling seed in rows
as mothers do. By yellow
lines, station to station,
we are needled, made
whole for the service
of death or culled
by codes we never know.

Under great casements of glass
pain appears in our knees.
Groins ache, blood clots.
We blink, swollen sheep,
butted joint to joint
down endless corridors
the fathers willed us.
Seeing at last what's
ahead some weep or go
rigid when a hammer falls
cold on the kneecap's brow.

Near dusk we piss at walls crude-dreamed
by boys who leave no name: the women
from Bosch's *Garden of Delights* or
plump enough for Rubens, put up
by aching arms that never had
paint or smelled flesh
suddenly ripe, who feared
the sergeant shouting to
press on, even as girls
swelled to hack the field
down, to raise it up again.

Runaway

Someone in the supermarket cuffs his child,
a young man with his lip gray
from his first mustache, his arms filled
with bread, milk, eggs, the father muttering

          'You'll pay for this, double

maybe,' and I hear anger's helplessness,
my father saying,
          'Go ahead. Be careful trouble
don't get you. Trouble likes a young boy.'

His age now, I know he means a boy gone
in the world the first time, little
change in his pocket, hard days, curbstone
for pillow, if lucky. Nobody to bother

about beds unmade, or bitch over the uncut grass.
I see my mother bent in her chair, sun
twisting her brown curls. I never guessed
those hands at her waist held back any pain.

I watch the smoke at his fingers, a restless line
that won't break until ash tumbles.
          'When
you get there write, give us some sign
you're making it, whichever way you end up,'

the final words I think he spoke – but maybe
also
   'You sleep on things.'
          Then nothing more
between us, except the night, and no one angry
for once, and her not screaming *Shut your face!*

Why is it sorrow I see, not anger? Hadn't I failed
my daily work, been churlish, hawked lies
he'd spit out with my name? Nailed
by his look, my mother follows him to bed.

Next day bacon, eggs, but not a single word
to stop me, and I want to ask about love
but can't as I eat in the light flared
through a dirty window. Dawn comes down the road.

I have come this far and I never asked him,
and he can't answer now. Except when
a boy I shout at trembles, his face a dream
troubled by shadows, shouts, my words lashing back –

'Go ahead. Run.'

The Chesapeake & Ohio Canal

Thick now with sludge from years of suburbs, with toys,
fenders, wine bottles, tampons, skeletons of possums,
edged by blankets of leaves, jellied wrappers unshakably
stuck to the scrub pines that somehow lift themselves
from the mossed wall of blockstone headlined a hundred
years back, this water is bruised as a shoe at Goodwill.
Its brown goes nowhere, neither does it remain, and elms
bend over its heavy back like patient fans, dreamlessly.
This is the death of hope's commerce, the death of cities
blank as winter light, the death of people who are gone
erratic and passive as summer's glittering water-skimmers.
Yet those two climbing that path like a single draft horse
saw the heart of the water break open only minutes ago,
and the rainbow trout walked its tail as if the evening
was only an offering in an unimaginable room where planes
inch ahead for the people, as if the trout always meant
to hang from their chain, to be borne through last shades
like a lure drawn carefully, deviously in the blue ache
of air that thickens still streets between brown walls.

Stroke

All the long days of years lying
alone the word feels pelt of rain,
shivers of night chill, and coils
in the box you built. It whimpers.

At first light it stands, stretches
to leash-length, digs a small hole,
having learned to wait, become what
through all seasons and all faces

you can't say. Eye-bristling, recalling
the down-spiral of leaves, flushed
wingbeats and sun's joy, you lie
flat in white yards of the clinic,

among victims in tunnels of shade.
The word scratches, paces, softly
drags its chain over the emptied
bowl, barks. You can't call it now.

It won't hunt for you. Penned, you
wait and listen to machines digging
steadily as nails in dirt, a hole
regrettable, too deep, unfillable.

Guinea Hens

They wait where the dirt lane unspools,
round and plump as mock oranges,
almost invisible in the black pines,
their thousands of pinched faces
all turning at once when I come home.
What have I forgotten to be that
my wife should seem in my head
here waiting among these watchers?

I lean on the wailing motorcycle,
a tide of whiskey unbalancing me,
thinking there may be only one,
her little heels like spurs, a shadow
of her wings floating suddenly past
the shaken headlight I can't control.
This happened. The night showed me
how things get tricky on roads where
a family is a river of tongues, a welter
of witnesses preening. What good is
hindsight? It hides, reveals each bump
and rut, flings down the bird scream
least expected, only for you to hear, savor,
then flee to heft the bottled, smirky
dark. Oh, lie once with wrong love,
you see how coming home means a pitched
chance of flight. Black, she screws
her grip on this place, her tongue says
you, you like a whip until, whatever
the world whines, surprise! It's her yet –
cackle, crow, rage, and wail – her
by morning's soft light nibbling, her.

Skunked

Under the womb-heavy wheezing of spruce
she finds him and calls until he slides out,
that big unhousebroken baby we lost.
I watch from an eclipse of floodlights
my wife kneel and try to coax this dog
into a rubber bowl shaped to feed
a sow strong-jawed as death, but he won't
stay, he's racing in the darkness,
stinking up the leaves he goes through.
It's midnight when the sluicing begins,
and her crying. He's still out there
long after the tomato juice has turned
her bath pink as the dawn, after we've

moved two states away, after snow sealed
in whatever expiations we gave ourselves.
Growing to be more than we could handle,
he won't return and we won't return.
We don't have photographs to show us
what happened. But when local dogs
howl like children, when thick summer
leaves us sleepless, oiled with sweat
like breast milk, I hear a snuffling
lift her and draw her out in her gown.
I see the red flow. I hear the spruce
groan at first spurts like desire, then
something lets go and we're rooting
in the black yard, calling out names,
boiling water, then waiting as we must,
telling ourselves whatever we have to do
it won't hurt and it won't stink forever.

Drag Race

Lying in bed I hear two come nose to nose
like fathers and sons, jockeying
in suburbs that want to rest in peace,
torque shaking the bodies
under the moonlight's eerie paint,
and the street shouts, goes
instantly alive with old arguments,
rubber's burning death-howl,
the mind peeling away into panic
as if the house breaks apart
like a flung melon, or a child's head.
I smell the honeysuckle that accepts
again, as it must, the awful
concussions of the ordinary, smoke
and oil, the quick snapping on
of houselights like fear
my father taught me to answer. Below
my dreaming it happens again,

a boy's hand drops the white flag
of a fist, striking the air
only, headlights lurch off together,
locked to the black horizon,
enough taunting voices to wrestle
forth the veterans, homeowners
half sleeping, also-rans of glory
shackled to crewcut lawns.
Over Japanese coupes like skates
their faces come out behind
curtains, worried, barely visible.
I could rise and walk among them,
my fatherly robe star-silvered,
unthreading with the age I bear.
I could say *sleep, it won't matter,*
not the dog's territorial wail,
not their boyish, belligerent cries,
not the beer bottles shattering,
not my father swinging the night
back to hunch up in my face,
sudden as his snarl I can't keep
from the scummy ditch where
love doesn't mean a damn thing.
I could call out *You!* to the boy
hiding in the sweet vines, certain
they'll pick him up as pledged,
secure in his head he isn't alone.
I could put my hand on him, make
him shiver this warm night
as his mouth sprays the outrageous
arguments of power. For us
I could say it's over, the black
streets all that's left,
saying go home now where love
tries to remember you. We might
stand so close and still the others
would believe we were learning
the secret of living together,
that paralysis of place
terrible and silent as nightmares
where porchlights flare on, off
inexplicable as combat almost

forgotten. In that light,
would he listen, clenched? Did we?
Don't lie, old man, he'd hiss,
just tell me what's going to happen.
Then, father, I'd push him,
say get away punk, run, try to live,
until they come back for you,
who are gone where the honeysuckle
throats still nod, soft, as if
they understand this night story.

Kitchen Windows

Because the house is too small, the season's
feast take the living room
for its abundant lounge,
a great turkey sliced on the stereo,
bowls of jellied yams, stringbeans, jazzy
stuffing only steps away by plate.
On the table there's chicken,
amber as the last leaves where we park,
and ham singed black,
with toothpicked red ribbons, pineapple
moons like a child's eyes,
a coffee urn with its strong blessing.
Some kneel, some talk. Atop
the television is corn bread, swaddled rolls,
infants of butter, red sauces,
sugar white as snow not here yet, promised.
An old college trunk has preserves
with that odd, eerie sheen
turned bright where television's on,
though no one watches
today's episode, the family soap's hacking
through the holiday fare
of sickness, betrayal, defeat, and the usual
edge of hope they leave
with the grade B cleanser's scum rinsed shiny.

Somewhere there's three
kingly decanters of wine, all domestic.
I walk back through these
rooms to praise what happens to us all,
heaped meals we juggle on knees,
childish as clowns, boffo tales
we tell each on another, breaking into song,
loosening our collared,
formal loves, shifting from wine
to harder things, arms flung now to anyone
suddenly there like an oak
still golden in a world slipped graveyard gray.
How is it we always wind up
in the kitchen, hammy hips on stainless steel,
cheeks booze-ruddy again
that winter will wash pale, smoke hanging
like youth layer on layer,
our butts sizzling out in the sink? I stop
here, coat off, sleeves up,
tight as a tick in the warmth of friends,
laughing through sweat
on my neck. Soon I will slide out the side
door and stand in the blue
breathhook of nightfall, that sorrow come back
to be forgiven again.
I step to the cool edge of stones at the alley,
not myself, but some other
spirit, benign, from a far wood, and stand
lit up, glowing inside
that long, cast-out hope of kitchen light,
as Chaucer, leaving court,
stood before a gorged family tavern to think
the night enormous and bitter
for so many, yet shadows
already danced, ludicrously brave, and so happy.

FROM **CUBA NIGHT**
(1990)

To Isle of Wight

As if owned by someone unshakable
inside me this tag-end white summer dawn,
I ride through Richmond over handlaid gray
cobblestones, passing porticoed houses,
locked iron fences of gentried shadows, pale
as their Anglican ancestors, then private
clubs where the only blacks are still waiting
tables, their faces smooth and innocent
as the dead gaze of Lee's looming statue.
A white man, tuxed, squints east at bloodless sun

straddling East Cary's one-way centerline.
I heave around him through Shockoe Bottom
where the state began: slaves, produce markets,
centuries of tobacco. Now boutiques, bars,
condos, all-night joints for lawyers cruising
after coke in Volvos. Here you pick up
Church Hill, passing under Patrick Henry's
impeccable shrine, street filth everywhere,
brick hulks the home of whores, winos, poor blacks
increasingly thumbed out, casualties

of developers in restoration.
Before Poe's stone cell I stop and put down
my car's top. St John's bells outshout the black
evangelist on my radio, but
he won't quit droning his sins, litanies
Richmond sleeps through, his congregation's ech-
o rising like death across the city.
Sunday mornings there's no music to calm
a man trying to find his way home – and
who hears the songs you have to sing alone?

At the mouth of Route 5, the plantation
road, I pass a graybeard who pees a wall
of antique stone. He waves without looking.
I go this back way to miss the families
piously crawling to the pillared church,
and shutter through sun and dreamy shade

Nat Turner held to when he rose in blood.
I smell the river the white houses keep
fenced off, invisible as the new South.
Sailing toward noon, I soon sag behind, then

pass, reckless with a free road, pickups whose
black drivers grin, wave. Now come Varina's
bunkered ranchers tucked down on treeless hills
that flatten to pine slopes, fields of soybeans,
rotting cars. I'm daydreaming and the air's
full of honeysuckle. Heat visible
as the whistling gleam of swords goes yellow
in sky open as a face freshly hacked.
Then it's blank country, nothing to be seen
but Charles City County's woods-wall and black

lanes where generations have passed in, out
like rain filling clay ruts. I ought to feel
fatigue, anger, something this land says. What?
I speed on, imagining back there
the slave-shacks hunching still with a peaceful
updrifting kitchen smoke and the wail of
a Sony's gospels. As remote from me
as foxhunting lawyers, the feet running
naked over that earth seem to whisper
as my tires pop head-bubbles of road tar.

Who lives here? Is it Turner's grim promise
in my skull hurting or the falling blades of sun
and buffets of shade? My radio's waltz?
Dark youths in a Comet flare past, fingers
lifted, light firing their windshield, weapons,
if any, hidden. The only war now
is personal, its battles always mute,
confused, enemies unnamed, slipping off,
abstract as Richmond's history. The bridge south
looms, wheels me over the thick, brackish James

to smokestack-sulfured skylines of Hopewell,
hopeless now as ghostly braves who here howled
for English blood on their hatchets, but saw
what Opechancanough dreamed: whites floating

upriver in gray ships, boiling out like
Mayflies hatched, too many to kill. They sang
for the end of things, died. Who hears them now?
An hour east land's flat, piney. Blocked-up shacks,
dead outhouses. Few leave this world. I'm near
home when I see stoops with setting faces,

sleepy over coffee, all habitual,
checking lanes where nothing but death happens.
Even the blacks are my kin at some point
I don't know, their stories mine in a speech
I once understood. Go past their doors,
their watching. Wave. Turn down a new-fenced lane.
Little's changed. Green greets me, fresh and firm
at once. It feels like an old argument
your kin meant not to raise because you've come
home where flesh is first. Summer heat boils.

Stopped, I smell the baking dirt. Like branding steel,
the sun leaves my back black with sweat. A shape
older than any shade I know, my age,
rises, comes warily as a yardhound.
I take his numbing toddy, drink, shake hands,
then sit to rock myself through rehearsals
of all the good times we've seen pissed away.
Everybody's dead, dying, or bad sick.
What did we want? 'You found out,' he says.
'Talk don't change shit. You live, work, die. You *die*!'

'Like blacks you want it all free. Life is deeds.
God's in real estate, not words. You got
dirt ahead.' Why don't we listen? We hack
like our fathers at lies, guilts, excuses
that don't show us why we go on failing.
Our words grow bitter as salt, louder.
Trapped in my brother's heat I drink and drift
with him through Vietnam, wars of Jews, Irish,
welfare, school's shit-books. 'You keep singing, Pal,
but whose life gets saved? Freedom's? You ain't real.'

What's home but arguments you can't escape?
Then more booze from his air-conditioned vault,

until we're rabbits hunched, fearing what barks
too close. I'm looking for holes to hide in,
swearing I have to go before night comes
when he points into his field: 'Look at her!'
Sudden as a snake's eye there's a woman
strutting a big horse, bareback, sweat-dulled flesh.
I watch her dismount in the deep green, swing
the reins loose and slap him to a gallop.

'Lord, whose angel is this?' I holler. Knee-
high when I looked last, his girl's bloomed with grace.
'Poison,' he sighs. She sits the topmost rail,
her sweater yellow as candleflame, brass
hair, long legs dangling from shorts gone mostly
to ravelled gray strings. Elegant as an egret
we shot one summer, crippled, crying out
as it swooped for cover. It watched from pines
while we blasted the gathering dark. 'More booze?'
he prods, ice clinking like fear, and I nod,

thinking *Sweetheart, it's only a matter
of time till they sing your song.* As if she
heard, a drumming starts, and steel guitars flare.
She swivels around, deep-tanned, arrogant
as sunrise. Grins. Lifts a radio
bound to her wrist. Beyond my kin bobs
the dark stud's huge head – as if he approves
this noise like pain spreading over dusk's fields.
'She sings with a band. All black except her.'
A cold voice grinds. 'That's them on her cassette.'

'You wouldn't believe the flies that honey
draws, country full of creeps. Like her mother,
she'll leave me. Thinks she's some secret goodness
the world wants. Ask me, can't be soon enough.'
I know before asking where. 'Says Richmond.'
I summon up dim images of Richmond's
sexless colonial houseladies, preppies
UDCs, westenders, club-wives – are these
the voices of the soul who will know her?

Music like a faith throbs against the dark.
I think of Shockoe's antique market, hands
clapping, laughter, the brazen dance of gold
girls leaving black and white faces amazed
in tobacco leaves, coiling to the sun.
My mouth's thick with booze like a slime of birth,
as if words almost burst to her music.
I squint in dead light to make my head see
what ghetto blasters say when young blacks roll
their eyes up, tuning the moon to old aches.

'Do you remember how we invented
words to be the indians who lived here?'
He glares, as if I'm from some cosmic zone
of otherness: 'Ain't none of them around.
We won that war, numb nuts.' We used to think
they kept living in these woods, we'd hear songs
we'd sing on our backs in bed. Didn't we?
'Kids grow up. Woods? It's pissy swamp. But mine.
It don't say a thing.' Now her voice breaks back,
drumless, raw, braiding speech to a steel beat.

'Thinks the heart's all you need to sing,' he spits.
The voice seems to speak inside me like fear,
I argue *maybe so*, aware bourbon's
sent its woozy courage straight to my tongue.
We sit past dusk, into blue dark, then night.
She vanishes from sight, though I watch her
by listening to the near-gospel of rock
she croons endlessly. She must love herself
to love us so, I think. Would I turn her
away if she banged my door? Say *Go home?*

They'll eat you! I want to say, but listen
to kamikaze bugs, then hooves like drums,
faint words I can't understand shrieked to one
sound as she swirls close, then disappears. I
mount up in a haze, shout goodbye, headlights
picking up an incoming load of boys
whose car thumps and sways past on cadenced waves
I begin to know. I remember my life
in the smell of this place as I turn back
on the hard road, snap the radio, then dial.

Out so far, I find only static's roar.
Houselights float past me like conjured torches
as I feel my speed increase. I could be
anywhere on earth. Nothing looks the same.
Nobody waves. It's dead Sunday. Deep night.
Then I see the county sign: Isle of Wight,
and I'm out, beyond the 'island of man',
running toward the city locked and silent.
This soothes me. Yet, alone, I want music
to enter me with songs, and dial the air

jammed with half-voices, zigzagging after
notes, overlapped phrases, my boozy soul
almost asleep when I find frequencies
fusing her with the black preacher I left
near Richmond. I can't tune either one out,
can't locate signals – as if one's ahead,
one's behind. Weaving, I look up at last,
shocked to see others on the road with me.
Black men leap from a hearse straddling the church
road that swerves into mine. Screaming love stops

pain, my preacher's too late. My face floats through
a woman's face planted on my windshield,
wanders into the sheared cries of a world
that pumps breath in my mouth. I'm down in clay,
kissed by moons of teeth. A man says 'Gon' die.'
Oh god, I hear them humming gospels, flashed
red light scorching me under him. I'm pinned
to a spruce, tasting blood. He says 'Don't ask,'
when one wants my name. Then, 'He Isle of Wight,'
and I hear them shuffle as if to leave.

No! I gasp against hands on me. *I'm kin!*
It's so quiet I can't tell who's listening.
Roots cut in my back like cast-off field tools;
I smell gouged dirt. Then I hear it: someone's
snapped her voice on in the wreck's heart. It soars.
Listen! I croak to draw the black breathers
back to my lips. *We can all sing like that.*
Faces swirl away, wind-wakes of passage.
Please listen, I cry. I know what she means.
Just let me up, just help me say the words.

170

Writing Spider

A path coils like the aphid's gouging the rose,
a dark line lingering by the finger beans.

No one sees me outrun the whiskered corn
or spill myself on the grass
or fall amazed under her silken staring.

Electric against the black law of the trees,
huge yellow zigzags around her
like lightning. A mystery, I think.

There's not yet the evidence we expect, swaddled
stingers, fuzzy cocoons well prepared –
but for whom? The web glistens.

I see the trunks leaning in, as if she draws them
with her tip-toeing strength. I rise,

pulling myself from under her without touching
or being touched, clothes a little clammy.
How old am I when I lift the stick,

prod this and that corner of her concentration?
It requires her to type back and forth
her swaying, signing possession.

I get very close and I do not believe
she has come to this revelation for me.
Or that she can jump

from time to time.

Crab House

Noon at the swamp's heart, the stink
falling from the smokestacks
cloaking the slender reeds that do not move.

Workboat's kapucka-kapucka pushes
the dark wave in over the mud,
then pulls it back so the skulls shine.

A gull settles onto a distant swell,
picks at white feathers like a German maid
in a sun-dappled bed. The sound of many legs

scraping against metal, the sound of water
boiling is in this air. I listen
as the swamp grinds its teeth, feeds, begins to reek.

Local Color

At low tide the mussels emerged moss-bearded,
necklaced gleamers along the ashen shanks
of a pier long abandoned to the mud's shimmer.
They gathered into clusters, pale-crowned

as stars coming out above December's slack waters.
One side of each was wholly given to darkness.
Nothing could change that, no lover's touch,
no atomic winter, none of the hammering waves

hurled from far out by no visible force – yet now
the sea went anonymously blue as the eye
of a beached fish, and the breeze charmed again
with that tang of salt you taste in fresh tears.

You could walk this lip of land and look close
where so many had nailed themselves to hold on,
just that, and it was the shell's primal black
you drew to, the ectoplasmic scorching of fire

in shades hidden by those bone-house skulls bent
to the only things their flesh would ever know.
Your life would not change for having seen this.
Gulls mocked the horizon and the seas bullied them

and ships swayed coming in and the shore hunched.
But, walking, you remembered that first color.
Beneath it, held by their ooze of yearning, things
moved like mutants over black wood, foot by foot.

2000

It's always been nineteen something for me.
Nineteen for my father all his life,
nineteen for my grandmother who went,
nineteen for my sister who wanders,
nineteen for my grandfathers who won't make it,
nineteen for my wife who will, our children,
and, for all I know, yours, and theirs.
Nineteen is a lot of sad, dirty numbers
and something that reports to none of us.

What good are words in the face of numbers?
They keep the shadow under a boat rotting
where I crawled as a child, they hide
the pitted spoon of dreams, they deliver
wind in tunes over the reed-heads of home.
They turn my father's face to a thin plank
where I cross the creek over fallen stars.
They are the zeros of sorrow something says.

I want to pick up my ears like a tired dog
when the whistling comes over the fences.
I want to lie down and dream of God counting
my sins until in anger he sounds sexual
as a Peterbilt diesel in a fishing scow.
I want to watch the words: nineteen something.
They'll loop out of sight like a slow worm
and I won't even try to read the slime,
the dirt, or the revolutions of the moon.

The Canoe in the Basement

Wanting to live in the world as it is,
I have tried to find your way.
Concrete walls, mossed a little, cool,
the room you dug below rafters
holds still that soft lap and slosh
of water where your carpenter
father came, breath in his toothgap
shrill, wanting to know why
you couldn't live in the usual house
like your neighbors, who stood
wiping away their tears of laughter.

*

'A foot down, anything floats,' he said.
'Even the dead know that.' But you
gouged underground by the Chesapeake Bay
a hole whose first concrete layers
seeped until the swamp's mucky oozing
spread like a fleshy brown butter.
Nobody knew why you refused to fill it
or where the canoe came from. The summer

I moved there, school just out, dawns
hammered the darkness back and I
dawdled like a dragonfly past the hacked
nibs of boards, down raw stairs
with your son, my age, who winked when
he said he'd show me your mistake.
We believed you could somehow lift up
and bend its womanly length, take
it like beauty through the raw framed
pine subfloors, but day by day
the walls closed in, and nothing changed.

I was patient. Years, it seems now, I
waited like a young Beowulf
dreaming inside the early sunlight
flashed through windows yet

unglassed, the bow-tick against stone
like the nudge of a steed's head.
But already I knew there was no other
water worse, its stillness not
still at all but a shifting pulse,
a scum, faintly red, greasy
at times like blood or a storm-sky.
Where was it pumping from?
Wordless, an acolyte, I watched you.

*

What alarms of enchantment, heroic,
comic at once, drummed you
to abandon your ordinary building?
Middle-aged, fat for the hull
you wedged yourself into, your wiry
gray hair going, you dipped
paddle, pulled, then crossed, recrossed
that slick darkness to begin
a rhythmic nudging against walls you
never escaped. Overhead, a wife
and children distant as the Pleiades
spooled in their lives. You
rose there at night, sailed at dawn.

No eye could see much in your life's
horizon, spiders, cocoons,
shiny killers in hard black shields,
but in this room-sized lagoon
I came to imagine the strange selves
I keep writing down. I learned
to listen as you beat a paddle into
awful melodies, garbled words,
tunes you banged out wall to wall. Once
you screamed 'Earl, you asshole,
you're drowning!' Hidden in azaleas,
ham sandwich in hand, I hurled
myself down through the jittery sun
and stood knee-deep while
you wailed for your would-be savior.

*

Years like slow bow-waves break, double
back, repeat, but I don't know
why the purple wisteria hangs sweet
or your dead voice calls out
like the quail at dusk. Your father,
laughing, swirled his hand
at his temple and we grinned, but was
this hope's illusion of voyage
or only our usual insanity of vision?
In the end the heaped plates
placed at stair-end gleamed, emptied,
the fat heart you had laboring
to carry you farther and farther off

like the slipping cadences of a craft
whose purpose is traversing
life's malignant, fathomless holes.
One of those you sent to bide
in the world, to report, when I go down
in my chair to write, I see you
begin to conceive it, the outrageous
boat proud upon the earth's
bloody upwelling, its carriage a soul's
indifferent to despair as to joy.
You would have visions, greet heroes,
sing the truth, accepting all
as it might come, benign, but not lost.

*

I remember the stout house you built
for the living, and the waters
that smelled like the uncoiled dead
had gathered to speak, the sun
spilling its endless road to truth.
I dreamed of canoes to keep one
sealed from the other. Yet all sink.
I tell myself still *Go forth!* When
my love cradles me in the dark, she asks
what is the future but a box,
brown, undulant, seeping away? I stop,
I listen, not dreaming. Your
face floats. Believer. A cold enigma.

Treading Clams at Egg Island

Among us the fathers labored like seals
and we would come behind them, crotch-
deep, tiptoeing the motherly waters,
each naked foot kicked out where sand
humped, darkness hiding its treasures,

then body's tumble and thrust to make
the fetal coil, to begin a weightless
grope downward through broken swells
of milky bottom. Opening the eyes,
we'd see weed-hair, polyps, big legs

before the salt's burning poured through
nerves and brain-stem. We'd convulse
head first from a shimmering cleft,
new muscles threshed by sun, matted
with the dead cells of old bar spawn.

Afternoons, floating with baskets, we
were catchers of the living and the dead
alike, oblivious, churning forward as
the tide washed us to a smell of dirt,
our lank place they called an island.

We learned to breathe hard and steady
as we opened them, knife-bulling,
the dangerous shove that risks slips
to the bone, praising the smaller,
least salty "cherrystones" not long

fallen from current's spurt and swell.
Walking over our people's garbage,
we'd gather to boast, to lie into fires
hidden by the cradles of sawgrass.
Houselights winked where water ended.

Fingering each mysterious seam, ridges
readable as a family line, grown
sleek, we were the muscles we loved.
Whatever we opened told us of more
out in the black water, so we plunged

to find the firm, sweet, angelic flesh,
scaring ourselves with the moon-steam
of our diving. Then, calling to stars,
the brothers of creation who made us,
singing aloud for the life we lifted up,

the salted, pink-lipped, slimed pumpers,
we grew sea-clotted, our stenchy skins
scaled and shining, and passed nightyards
with old boats lying moon-weighted, open
as if they were dreams unfinished. There, we

stood like our fathers. Our baskets down,
we'd fight some, shout the dead awake.
We would wait. Already there'd be women
afoot in the levels of darkness, stirred
to venerate what we caught, what they caught.

Pillage

The sun has done eternal damage, pine warped
to the white, arthritic shins of men. Here
they shouldered hung come-alongs and galled
harnesses, they led out the heavy striders
of meadows and later stood counting the green
strings of hunger as they passed the tall door.
Here are roofholders they raised, gray beams
axed from an infinite country's brood, and ribs,
struts, planks, overlapped, darkened by time.
Against the back wall startled wings beat,
noting our presence, stirring the rich silts
of the world that lives here now, the silence
unmocked by our loud crying out. In a frieze
of webs a shadow moves and we feel ourselves
placed in shafts of light, trespassers driven
from desire to fear in this abandoned barn.
Why are we here? we ask aloud, as if the dead
wood knows, unimpeachable as nests of swallows.

178

But even Prince Albert stays speechless, canned
at dirt-shrouded windows we can't budge. What
do we want badly enough to risk this stealing
under the cathedral roof? Something black seems
alert above as we back toward the August light
and pass beyond the scaled foundation stones
hand-laid like a language we once understood.
Then out, we are chilled in the sun, the smell
of ourselves oddly imprecise yet powerful
as a memory of passion when we stand alone
remembering how we crept in, how we burst out,
our hands filled with cowbells, straps, tools,
relics for mantels in our bright, modern houses.
Agreeing to return some Sunday, already we
make up tales to explain why we never go back.

Welders

Behind us, at the window, my grandmother
stood with death's fat grinding her down.
Today all I have of her is the stone
grave, the ground we loved for pines
swaying through hammered Sunday sermons.

Here the booming day-long traffic darts
like the dead's souls embarking, spits
of light from windshields burning away
the last green where she was put in.
That summer they meant to teach me desire

would lead to lingering pain, blindness,
the cost of making things go together.
I stood near grandfather's dark place,
full size in fig's shadow of green,
still as an acolyte, his pricking stream

of light motes turning the world in my head
molten as July's flare. 'You look aside,
you see...' But I disobeyed and stared.
Black-cowled he hunched, became a monster,
a gargoyle scowling, a bent breath-sizzler

whose hands cradled swamp-fog and fire.
Was this the chest I had slept on
to hear the histories of our names?
A nerve in my brain turned phosphor
until I went faint among the needles.

What was he making? Rabbit-trap, the last
beauty-catcher for her? The bright gutter
she watched, the spurt and lick of life
blistering those who gaze into black
distances – that's all we keep. In a heap

somewhere whatever it was still moulders,
not the astonishing moment of a maker's
clang and bang of vision. Nothing.
Then the hand touching. How much?
I imagine the faces who look at it,

blank, as if all is only to be embedded
in silence, ignorance, season's passage.
As if knuckles of steel did not speak.
Days then her hands cooled my forehead.
Light sizzled and we went on, making.

Lake Drummond Dream

For we are not pans and barrows...
RALPH WALDO EMERSON

Reading Emerson. Cottonmouths are moving mildly
in swamp midden, the whip
of nerve-spurred flesh
going down, glints

incidental in the rolling fume of darkness
where the moon fingers like thought
and eases around the rib-cage
of beauty. To find life

in the eye's cleavage: a spread spiralling water
gone still, sudden. Puddle in back yard,
the standing scum. Depth unexpected
in all things, the striking

quickness of the afternoon overhead, remembered,
and not to be able to confess the name,
the nature of what marries all.
Then, the self sitting

stiller than the sparrowhawk inside his glance,
already owning, without awareness,
small wings. Dreaming of home,
the lake, spine-sliders,

not expecting to touch, across the library desk,
a woman's hand, finding it dry, cool,
eyes shocked open, all
the darkness around

uncurled from deep texts of matter. Know it comes,
hear, touch time's announcement. Plant
the feet on the floor's waterskin.
Try to know the unavoidable

thing, meeting its depth.

On Looking into Neruda's *Memoirs*

At the end of Elliewood Avenue one black night
the police came whirling batons
to crack heads and leave
the students in the seeping flush
of camellias that Spring.

A woman found me and into the riot we went, me
tugged by the ghost-tendril of her arm,
bolting by the tidy lawns until down
we lay at the serpentine wall,
panting, in new music

beating from an open window – 'The Famous Flames'
maybe, but she was cool, wordless, alert
as a dove to the night noise.

She uncradled her hungers in the dark, then rose
lank as the poet Gabriela Mistral,
whom Neruda saw in his youth.
He called her gray stick,
as if she were the heron
owning the world with icy steps.

Why has she waited to enter this poem, a small
scald at my brain's back?
Whatever she put in my hand
was grim and hard in the heaving.
Go on, show them, she said, *give them a taste.*

She hovered on the corner, a tall shadow.
When they came to beat me she stepped away
through helmeted heads, a saint
with an eye of disdain
for all my earnest words.

It doesn't matter, the dutiful life, the poems.
A man will complain for his first loves,
brick smell, lost village, sexual
odor of swamps, the scarf
of a nightwalker, a single camellia.

Mistral, who worshipped the long-stick God
of the Crusaders, kneeled in the huts
where Neruda grew. He saw her
once, enough,
a stick making poems.

Bitch, you almost hear him hiss,
pressing her hard in the story of his life.

Camellias

Something with claws, with trap-spring teeth
honed, shining where leaves peel
back from midnight's folds,
is intent and desperate beyond
the imagination where I look,
howled awake: a few
luscious petals suddenly are shaken,
so I think guilt always
keeps just behind the heart.
In beauty something is jerking a small other
apart, breaking the slight bones,
the cross-stitched sinews,
its tongue drawn like a shaving knife, abandoned
where it hunches. Nothing answers
either, only the silence hiding
the scream that came,
pitiful as the nightmare in the ear
of the lover. It is
no decent hour but I ease from my bed's cool,
step down the blind corridor
with my nakedness swaying, then
paw for the switch. Harms I might do rise
like a fester of wings when I throw
the light of revelation over our backyards,
into bedrooms. What makes me
heave it as indifferently as a hunting sun?

Instantly something clenches
the earth, digs in, doesn't
bolt, lifts itself to see, mouth partly open,
the tiny tongue in throat-black,
and throat as well, disguised but pink
as the unfolded, dewy crenelations
of camellias uncountably opening
themselves in seasons
pure as Florida. It is all framed
by the flawless black meat and fur coiled
upon itself like night-after-night.

On a Quilt in the Bennington College Library

What should we see in this artifact? Incredible
colors, yet not so stunning as the peasant girl
seen once, perhaps, by her maker, cheek-red
and eye-blue pure, as if frozen in hope's dream.
We're always driven to demand from the useless
beauty that stares us down: what do you serve?
This white was a pet goat's inner thigh. Love's
lesson tells us to covet well whatever stinks.
Isn't it lessons we've come for? Pretty is
as pretty does, this tidy architecture says,
its squares like houses stitched in firm.
A village of cloth American as a Currier & Ives.

But this too-perfect Puritan fantasy rankles,
moves us back, forward to focus, find the room
with that girl ended in some posture of abandon
near the piss-pot toppled to a reeking stain.
From the shadows of books comes the dying cough
of a dreamer. A chair scrapes like a scream.
Who bursts past into the light? We look back,
see a patch left off-angle like a troubled
face whose question has one answer replicated
endlessly: faith. Our eye follows little fences
of thread binding all a house gets. If fear
makes us hang up pretty pictures, art invites

pain to show us what we know we'll lie under –
the first soft gargle of blood at a goat's slit
throat, the pus sealing a baby blind, a girl
who measures her years by the stones shoveled
aside for the bodies she's put into the dirt.
Where is she, the one who fled under ribbons
of punk-wood smoke, choosing the black rain
with only this homemade skin to surround her,
until God's voice in a spruce sent her home?
Hung here, the quilt's a shapeless play-pretty,
American abstract, survivor of no one's evil.
They've nailed it up in the air, out of reach
of the sun that remembers the bed, the woman
groaning and bleeding until she was colorless,
a dark space no one looked at or questioned.

Cuba Night

The small of the back has its answers
for all our wrong turns, even the slightest,
those aches there's no name for, or source,
and the mole in the mirror, a black moon
of sudden importance, can turn your hours
into love's rapt attention. As you shave
an innocent glance into the yard pulls
your lips mulishly – is anything there
more than a choice, a will to live? When

the fly on its back, feet up in dead air
between the storm-doubled panes, stiffens
it seems a reminder redolent of a word
you can't speak, like history, but feel
as once you felt the shuffle and slap
of your father's feet on heartwood floors.
He would be bathed then, as you are now,
unshirted, coffee starting, his lathered
clownish cheeks white, the dawn oozing red.

Quizzical, you hear the razor pull closer,
strokes deliberate, hard, almost independent.
Is it death? Only a café memory, you two
standing outside, soft night, a radio,
Kennedy declaring over the dirt his one
line only a war could cross. Your mother
wasn't yet meat that a drunk's Ford would
leave in a frogspawn ditch. Then your father
stopped to visit, shy, held your teenage hand,

while along the block many leaned, listening.
Dusk steadily bled all the light from each
face, a voice – maybe Bob Dylan's – said this
is history, and you said what? Same word
when your wife cried I can't stand any more,
whose crying had started under your yes, yes.
You can't smell her stale sheets and no
memory's kiss mushrooms. No late show's
rerun of Bikini atoll keeps flaring at you.

What then? Only azaleas beginning to explode
that must have been planted in that year,
the smudged hand now earth's, with questions
he couldn't answer. His eyes brimmed wetly.
Nobody you know's been to Cuba or cries out
what history means. There's blood on your lip.
The mole has grown. You're starting over,
remembering the floor that seemed to shake
with their love, then with the unslipping of
her nakedness, soap-white. Then the shaving.

A Pinto Mare

Mud packing her gullet the robin pecks
at winter-withered grass, black eye
cocked, serene as a man I saw bent
at a radar screen's blipless blue. His
lips spread on a mouthful of pizza
as the end of the world settles, a joke
I took home when my duty was done. Now

186

just beyond my window the thunder booms
Spring at this scruffy, fearless bird.
There's no worm and no nest in sight –
what makes her keep on, rain misting
through trees slick as missiles? She
rips, skips, tears hunks of the earth,
a nerve dutifully alert to what day is.

Years ago, just married, I walked with
sun napalming a field's face where
tinfoil the landlord hung flashed out
against crows, a sound like far swords.
The robins worked, humorless legions
of fathers, mothers, barely lifting
themselves from shadow to shadow and I

found the pinto mare with the half-born
foal: its black, dirt-clotted nostrils,
the short-haired head all night bobbing,
unable to bring its body forth. I thought
Christ, the son of a bitch landlord again,
asleep, drunk, his unattended toys blown
into death, drifting off without a sound.

Across the pasture the stud's big head
pumped up and down, broad ass scratching
a post as he watched us. Gimpy himself,
he turned away, trotted to deeper green,
one muzzle-muffled snort smart in the air.
Rage? What could he do, or me, or you?
Phantom F-4s from Langley shot overhead.

I wanted to throw rocks, shout, to fist
the sky with anger. Head-down the robins
patiently worked the mud, so I put one
hand on the leathery cheek of the foal
and the other on the pinto's warm rump.
That black eye stuck open, fly-specked,
gleamed when I squatted to look inside.

The past? The future? A small mistake made
in breeding? – I wanted to ask, but the mare
stepped on, head just above the grass-tips,
hunching, trying to eat. Robins waddled in
her smelly wake. I heard her teeth grinding
the small-skull rocks, indifferent to me,
as her spittle cut dirt, chewing the sun.

Loneliness

Trying to sleep off loneliness,
    I wake and stare at space.
Then I see the helpless gifts
    we give, our family face

the darkness will rend and chew,
    no reasons deducible.
Why am I me? Who begets who?
    Absurdity's tautological

as the mind's emptiness that lies
    between our children,
dreaming in upper rooms, and us.
    I wake with the wind

banging around the loosened glass
    of storm doors I locked.
The cold front's predicted mess
    announces itself, socks

each flank of our blackened house.
    The kids will wake alone
one day, in snowlight or sheet ice.
    We won't tell them to go

play on useless courts, build men
    of water that falls sick
with acid. Have I dreamed them, spent
    on dull books, who'll trek

off, not unhappy, to engender
  sorrow's black seeds again?
Suddenly middle-aged, provider
  of their death, in this wind

I try to feel this puzzle out,
  eyes fixed past the ceiling –
what stays, what goes in the howl
  of storm dizzying me

back to faces I love and forget
  like lessons. In snow's wail
I see my children, shapes who drift.
  They play basketball

and I'm among them, moving ghostly
  under freezing streetlight.
My father once played above me,
  in a float of breath-bright

leaping that lifted me to his heart.
  Then we went filing in
to wash, eat, sleep – to lie apart
  not dreaming it could end.

But snow kept us inside, or rain.
  Then one of us got sick.
Then? I hear my boy get up, drain
  himself, the floor-creak...

I listen to the flush trickle
  away like blood from my
house, my parents risen, middle
  of the night. Do they

cough, pad somewhere still? I don't hear
  their promise of heaven,
only the blurring days that smear
  ice on the glass, vision,

what's left of it, the future's guess.
  How little must be known
by the dead waiting, like lost gifts,
  dreamed by their abandoned

children, who pass them on in turn
   in names, words, photographs
someone has to explain. Disinterred,
   the past grins. Mute. Past.

Nothing we do can make it speak
   the joy it wanted, and gave.
Why am I one who hears, in grief,
   the deadly silence they have

reached? Their faces come back shy,
   agape around our beds –
light-glints, sleet. Nothing's said. I
   am becoming the dead

I will be soon. Sand-trucks spray
   our street. Under the hoop
I wish my children's children to play,
   but see them there stooped,

elders in my mind's weight, snow's hush
   like backache at their skulls.
They try to know what we wanted, flush
   in the moon, playing ball,

and seem almost to pray, as if they
   think us near. We are the noise
of weather under roofs that cry
   to them now, their joys

who dribbled in moonlight once. Afraid,
   I see how Adam went
down, a man, and night came. Eve cried,
   then followed. Each soul lent

the dark his face. Heard. The eternal
   numbing storms, the gusts,
morning's ice-sleep, then God's awful
   gift of loneliness.

Deer in the Yard

The odd, false rain of ice melting from leaves
brown and sodden in the elms lifts my head
as dawn arrives indifferent and still. Before me

sheets of paper lie. The hasty, unremembered
arrowings of intention cluster and argue.
Once I thought I had seen a meandering buck's

white tail near the broken swings. Probing
the dog-yellowed snow for new shoots, maybe.
He'd have to be sick, desperate, I thought.

Eleven or so, voices barking out everywhere,
moon like a searchlight. The late news flared
on my wife's sleeping face down the hall, past

unread letters, a stack of dull suburban poems.
What matters to anyone, I thought, in a deer
I may or may not have seen? All night, the ice

like my intentions mounted up, sealing life in,
not pure, but ugly as this moment freezing spit
I send from our steps, a little defiance. I am

groggy with my heart's attack, fear and age
like a fist. Behind me the news says Israelis
shot a young Palestinian mother in the back.

Blank as a recruit, gun in hand, I wait. Why?
Ice crusts the picnic table, the Jesus tree,
the first redbuds in the back where I saw him.

Gargoyle

I used to walk that sidewalk in your head
where, in the middle of one block,
the house rose, shabby as a lion out
of the dust, windows glazed with a filth

offering no explanation. Over the door
what must have been a hand's
long-practiced dream appeared every day,
though it had no name, the head
poking itself into the raucous pleasure
along our street, cruising,
its layers of paint like a whore's makeup
shocking, but in the rain sad
as the blank eyes tried to blink it all off.
It was always there, nobody looking,
nobody asking who made this thing,
no answer but the traffic. This was not art,
only the crude moves of thick fingers
that now I think may already be gone from us,
as almost certainly the beast is
cut down who leaped many times in my sleep,
who once hovered in a deep nightmare
I walked into, with a woman dead
and someone skinned-up, weeping.
The people had seen and gathered to watch.
When they walked away, her eye
dark as a window cradled in my hands, but I
could not see what it saw every day.
You could go with me to ask the thick fingers
what it all meant, if we could find them,
But I think even the corrosive smell
of mildew under the house where we lay together
once wouldn't answer. I think
the beast whose body kept hidden in the wall
is only the shape of change, is
gone, the walls are gone, and you and I are
going to walk up our street grown
fully, swaggering, collars open, speaking loud
where it all happened. The truth is
the others there with us will not understand
why we are as we are with no cause
visible, our eyes blinking, and no clear reason
to fear the past's untranslated
beasts, the present's tongue-tied selves.

Southern Crescent

The Crescent Limited...will...cross the wide
stream of the stately Potomac, pass the historic
spot where the best blood of the country
was poured in its great civil strife...
RICHMOND & DANVILLE RAILROAD BROCHURE, 1891

1.

The Crescent, silver as tinsel in vacant lots,
pistons through dawn-glow
and corrugated roofs ripped
from rowhouses by the bums,
the heaped poor, the dead
mounting up behind
bushes and bandoliered windows. A few

blinks is all it takes and you're gone
past black limousines, Washington's
monuments, traffic, fields once
green now the vomit
of rust, wormy dog-bodies,
spraycanned annunciations
of glory in garbage that won't quit,

slimy mattresses, asylums of fires,
disemboweled dolls, beercans,
endless black Os of tires
like breath's bubbles
on dead lips. Then
plywooded warehouses,
streets empty, brickpiles,
scrofuloid, ashen ditchbanks
and scum oozing. Who lives here

but those you want left behind? The unseen
cook in tents pitched of clothes
by track-beds. They hide
to ache alive and you
pass through them
like memories they can't stop.

A face wrapped in gaudy Christmas paper
flattened on cheap linoleum, spit
puddled. The eyes have floated
open, opaque as plexiglass.
They want to stay open.
But what do you want?

Sleepers, celebrants, sink in every seat
around you, their smells jostling.
You grope for your wife's hand.

2

My wife's dead father gazes at me from her
lids fluttering open on the window.
She sleeps upright, perfectly
composed, new-born, dazed.
Her lips move. I see
flesh stain on the glass,
the smear of all
we are: meat, skin, oil.

What is she trying to say? Did he tell her
long back, still alive in her breath,
something coal-acrid, smelly
as the abandoned
Pennsylvania house?
Is it despair's *No*, and *no*?

When her foot trembles it is
like a child's, cold, thrust outside
the frayed blanket in the soulless room.

I don't care if it's Christmas.
He's my father. I can't stop
remembering his smell
on my sweaters.
I have to go to him.
I can't help it you hated him.

194

A huge hand shaking my shoulder marries
me to this moment, punches my
tickets home. How unreal
death makes anything
we know: I wander
in my mind to pines
we lived under, sun
in the needles. They are
concrete malls, drifting knots
of paper. Gone. Just nowhere.

But beyond the gray hill-rims, past
my wife's head that has toppled
again, the day heats up.

Her feet, shoeless, rest on the cardboard
box she put him in, the urn
unremarkable as garbage

or pawned memento of a man's living.

3

He couldn't help the drinking, I say.
We switch sides, trying to know
what, who to forgive.

Out of the pastel parlor, out of hearing by his
priest dressed like a hip dentist,
we walked in the snow-spit.
I tried to say he was
only a man. Like us.
He loved what
he knew how to love.

Himself?

Yes. But not well,
so long alone, the priest said.

And me?

Better. You always called, talked to him.

What the hell do you think love is? Words?

Decorating the tree, we got slowly drunk
with gin left in his thermos.
We made love, hunched
like cats, curled
on the floor where
he sold the pot-belly,
and passed out,
and died.

*I don't know where home is now. A place
is just a sound where people
stay alive.*

OK.
We'll take him with us.

    4

Her lips move as if to answer something asked.
It may be the shock of the earth,
stones, mounds of decay,
debris our tracks
heave through.

They make breath's incomprehensible whistle.

Then I see the river we cross,
gray flats, a white crane,
austere, lifting off
alone. The grayer
swoop of the hawk
drops into reeds
without sound or notice.

On the other side we slow before a shack
cluttered with life's junk. Steam
gilds the tin roof where
an old man, shirtless,

red-faced on his stoop,
hangs diapers, grins,
and lifts to me
his horny middle finger.

'Merry Christmas,' that mouth says.

Crawling ahead, helplessly I laugh
until we clatter faster, faster –
the world pushing my head back.
What had been on her father's
lips softly
uttered as he fell,
no one even to rasp What?

What name did he have for love?
I know what he called my wife,
the way he drank and went on
dying, begging her to come home.

  5

When I lean to kiss you
I am full of the words
the dead have spoken,
mouths slack and dry,
wanting the name
for the little
we know enough to love.

Shacks whip by,
weathered, peeling, gray
as the horizon. But each
breathes a punky smoke.

Somewhere inside a child
grinds through 'Silent Night'.

I blink at that finger erect in air
until I see behind it on the shack door
Christmas bulbs. They fade then
wink back as we pass,

living and dying together.
You wake and smile.

What is it?

I tell you about the old man
giving me the finger, his lights.
I couldn't help myself laughing.
His living in human shit,
his lights.

They winked.
Like he was waiting for the world
he hated.

Or loved?

Yes.

And we showed up. We were it?

Yes.

*Just heading home on the Crescent
this happened?*

Yes. It seemed enough.

And that's all there was?

Yes.

You mean all you could see.

Yes.

NIGHT PLEASURES

(1992)

The History of the Queen City Hotel

Il ricordo e lucignolo...
MONTALE

When the children ask where we come from,
I start here, our tales of the South.

Nights, maybe our fists and cheeks bloodied
on each other, we'd pass their brick walks
and lay down and try to dream.
The blue hydrangeas, moon-whitened,
held their houses close. They watched us.

There, we knew, if we lived
it would be years of rooms lined
with newspaper for heat, smoke rancid,
staring at rain-smears on the ceiling –

a map where those before us went,
until they stuck, faces
in mud, snow-swept streets.
Running, what blessed thing had they changed?

That's how you come to the new place, you slip off,
clutching the letter that lies how better
everything is, your body aches in rooms
of the dark fouled with men. Cousins, strangers.

*

A young woman was bent, sobbing, they gaffed her
with their fists, their uniforms glinted
under gaslights, under the stars.
As I passed she touched me.
I knew I would fight them for her.
They called us trash, garbage,
shit-whelp of losers.

How odd to feel kinned to a stranger known only
by suffering, that thin thing in the eyes.

*

'Let's go,' one said afterward.
He might have been my brother, just older
by a week or a year, a dark foreigner.

'You call me Uncle,' he said.
A black canvas coat, soft drawl.

With that one, now dead, I slipped
to the shadows of the Queen City Hotel.
A bottle clinked on him, too loud.
The night made me feel underwater.

I could see the moon-faces inside, pale boys,
fire-haulers, gandies for the trains,
white plates like planets, steaming
with beans, meat, good bread.

I thought: I will eat meat on that china.
My head was drunk with possibility.

                    *

When my dead uncle flipped into the coop
his looped string with hooked corn,
waiting – was it a lifetime? – for nibbles
it was all wings flapping, blizzards
of feathers like ghosts shot over,
and the chicken, Oh Jesus,
make it stop hollering...

And his rock fell and the yakking stopped.
And I stopped breathing the air, shriek-strung.
And we soon spoke louder on pine paths
as if they were carpets
where the rich lived.

And I saw with that uncle, I could go anywhere.
Useless brass locks, useless cops.

                    *

His fire held a river, we drank its sweet red flow,
singing songs to honor the shadows running,
the dead one said, like us, for hope.
'Or at least, fresh chicken.'
He made me promise to remember
even stars floating in our coffee.

This was before the Hotel burned,
before I was hurt bad by the Depression,
before love that made you stepped among us.

On that night I drank my first whiskey.
I ran. I felt free.

Blowfish and Mudtoad

Held casually, either can deform who you are.
Hooked, furious, bubbling visions, they
float up clamped, groaning their truth,
rows of teeth serrated as ritual knives.
Moss-covered like bottom rocks, trailing
brown saltwater scum, current-fluttered
flags of weed, eyes like glass pitted by age,
each reads closely the downdrifted offerings
it waits to eat: fins, worms, wings, garbage
the great flow gathers to sweep away at last.
Our line flung into that steep wants sleek
ones to claim us – big Blue, Striper, Thor-Drum.
But first come dark's ironheaded preachers:
Blowfish, chicken of the sea, sly breather,
Mudtoad, black mouth chopping at the sun,
names spit out with care, a family's, our own.

At the Greek's Bar
(*Williamsburg, Virginia*)

Heavy tables, wood gouged with names, some dead on ridges
    in Korea, booths yet bearing their hot tunes
        on wall-boxes for music (night flares
            in cheek-to-cheek dreams),
                a boy like me

        woke alive, the flash of her exploding red
    cardigan hooked his eye, she no more than the thin
thrush singing down Gloucester Street. On his arm
        then, no moves impossible, beer-scum floor
            dragging like deep snow,
                but nights

        prickle the skin like a rash. Place memory:
    bolt, dance, sweat for the joy lost. Your father found
your mother here. Your name was with the Greeks. *Before.*

        Before what?
                Vietnam.

Jujubes

Inside the movie, sunk in hard hair seats creaking
    with fear, we learned life happened
in black and white, a redemption of wars. Horse-thrown
    braves, marines snipered by Japs in trees,
all those who lied and didn't look like us got paid the same.

Girls huddled in this flickering. The sticky aisle stayed
    patrolled as death by death we soaked up how
the hero, moral, defiant, vengeful took on any number of
    others, laying down the laws we were heir to:
No cigarettes, no booze, no bikinis, not a single Trojan

horse with its gentle deceit. What could words have told us?
    Soon we'd swim naked at the Y. But first dark
days, fake fruits, sucking the nipples, and box after box
    of empties sailed like sharp-eared bats.
Nothing would taste so good again, be so sweetly colored.

Pulling a Pig's Tail

The feel of it was hairy and coarse
like new rope in Johnson's store,
and I'd never touched any part
of a pig until that day
my father took me to farm ground
where he grew, the woods
a kind of moving stillness, green
hanging all over. I felt I was
underwater and should be
swimming for my life, not walking
up and down rows until we
found pigs huddled. The farmer, my
Uncle Bern, said one was mine
if I could catch him. A little one
looked easy, my size, but
wary, uncertain about many things,
the way he darted all ways
at once. I chased him while foul mud
covered me, the farmers laughing
through tears of joy, scooting out
to head us one way, another, all
wanting to see I could catch
what my father had, and his father,
like a faith in the wood-dark
self I had never even seen.
I called but it did not listen, then
tired, or scared, I don't know,
it slowed and I took a grip, I pulled,
both of us grunting in shit
like bad dreams. Why didn't he bite?

I heard them holler I had him,
the thing gone straight, but I saw
no end to what I now held, let
go, cried. My father smoked, they said
what's life like by the ocean?
I was thinking about my teacher who
yanked my hair when I kicked
the girl who said I talked funny.
I wanted to tell my father ·
a pig's tail burns your hand when you
can't let go, and I wanted to go
where we lived, the waters
spread out like a clean, fresh world.
I knew I would sleep by him,
my smell a new shadow in his clothes.

Basement Waltz

Probably the Platters, first music
        to beckon inside, pushing my legs,
arms, confused spinal cord – who
        knows what beat up and down, the tap
my foot took by itself working up
        until all of me trembled the way
        a man starving will shove his face
flush in the garbage. And she,
        tulip slender, has time left her
        now dumping the day's debris, cat
twining her sweet ankles? Where howls
        that starflare of her
        eyes, lost in what shadow of pain?
I want it to lift and walk me back
        across a black basement room, the slash
light lays down the stairs like a path
        no one has taken yet. I see rooms
we bruised ourselves in, breath and sweat,
        buckled floorboards heaving, a dance

getting faster as we fly apart − as if we
    must stomp some lower darkness off
before it climbs around us. Where,
        just when I closed to kiss her,
went the word the Platters stopped singing? It
    might help me say how in my head
she has slumped helplessly in my arms,
      and I don't know what to do
    with her, I have to wait, hear her
breath against my ear, the word: it dips
    like an evening bat, knows, goes, slick
in air as a mother's cheek after you
    learned you must kiss her
      in the silk box. I think if I
could sing what the last loving word was,
  it might beat back from that hole all
who wait, starting to sway. Looking up.

Burning Pine Straw

Eisenhower's bungalows where I lived
humped over cars like turtles, one to a driveway,
no new chain-link fence yet ours in hammered sun,

pine straw red as Mrs Berman's hair
drifting and blurring the line between our yards.
I was told to keep this clean. *Yard-boy,*

she called me, teasing, not like my father.
Over that straw whispering she stepped, my dream
with her high breasts, muse of drool I slept in.

Which among us could so have hurt her?
Had some demented son beat her and bit her,
who'd curl naked in her yard, a crushed beer can?

My father said to help. I carried trash,
walked her small dog with a bow down the line
where the straw thickened, oozing onto our street.

Cars blew it back on us when they passed.
I understood my father who wanted it raked, burned,
that uncivil mess, but not her, ranting out at us,

convinced the smoke came from bodies boiling
where we had never been. When they took her away,
my father said *Good. She's crazy. Now cut the grass.*

All summer the pines kept deep green, only
first red needles muffling the ground that soon
storms, nightwinds, quick freezes would matt

like dead hair in a damp box. Pulling
the needle-weave to fire I found white roots,
green still tender in October light. No one screamed

at smoke filling up rooms, blackening clothes.
No one came out, lay hand on my arm, cried, begged me
to come home, who was no one's husband long vanished

as now, Fall dark stirs, summer bleeds away.
Where do they go? Fathers, neighbors, smoke split
by Spring's red birds just moved near our yard, singing?

The Egret Tree

Ghosts of our fathers flocking down at dusk,
    one by one you return and stand
    shouldering the dim western light. Limbs
      you stride, live oak chambers,
  creak with hundreds of you, white-robed,
      abrupt as stars, or the flared

      windows of offices where clerks gird
for war, lawyers blue-eyed, in impeccable suits, who
      peck in their own endless documents.
          What do our people need?
      Dusk-wind sifts the tree moss like a beard
        in its fingers. Over the lake's

lull, past black roofs where some bend above meals,
    you descend as if elected to this day,
    summoned brother by brother down, the tree
        burning with starlight you bring.
    Night lowers black-winged as we pass car
        after car, penitents once, now

      townsmen only, bareheaded, surprised you are
among us, leaving cars, standing, making our chorus
        of oohs, ahs greet each new arrival.
          Some obligation or need
    spills us here, in peace jamming sidewalks,
        roads, freeway. Almost we feel

panic begin. Cries for help. A curse on your kind.
    Do you hear it? The cop's kick stand
    snaps, his cycle gouges dirt, blood's dark
        oil squirts but we won't move.
  We want what keeps you so calm. Little
        wonder water fills with *Amens*

      weaving the burst last red spatter of sun.
Sirens knife our breath. The stilled waters tremble
      as we listen, trying to remember
        how fabulous love is, and you,
    brightness, holding a tree rooted in the mind's
        hunger, the lake's ooze.

Out Whistling

Driving home I see the white heron on one leg
    yards out in the lake, like a woman
sun-glazed, dreaming next to a seaside rail.
    The lifted knee, down-delicate, holds
light in my mind so I drive around the block

to find its black eye again. The little globe
    orbits with me, hidden in my car,
all of us waiting, and traffic steadily rasps
    like breath over cancered tissue.
What did you want from me? No ripple comes as

one leg replaces another, the eye satin, hard
    with sun's burning. So much
of us flashes there I remember a wind's flare,
    an instant, your cigarette, a street
you crossed to find me when I was out whistling.

Wreckage at Lake Ponchartrain

Baton Rouge to New Orleans, hauling Route 10, workweek
    done, flying home with old tunes booming,
        road jolts, shaken by the bodies,
I come into the room of a long wood quiet as a parlor.

Wisps of moss like an elder's beard. I fly by two snug
    grandmothers in a Chrysler. Miles later
        I'm shamed by the glare of their
pouchy lipsticked fear, a melted look I see some dawns.

Whose is that law of the eyes? I turn loud 'Go Johnny go,'
    pop a beer, grin. Then I slow down to watch
        the insweeping lake, a carpet
stinky and black and giving under its crane stepping ashore.

Brown Shoes

Today in the airport, baggy
bloodshot antithesis of crisp
suits with gray news, those
makers of final decisions,
I stood in the rings made
by their long cigarettes,
with mothers in the tiered
sun like a hothouse calm.
Each looked far past children
in the jetroar and the carts
wailing the handicapped away.
Beyond old ones the hot glare
of runways gave back the black
engines pushing the reluctant
hulks to go, while here men
waved their arms, gesturing
as if to explain it all,
then turned aside, silenced.
I felt the building shake
when someone left unseen.
The children played harder,
abandoned to skylines of glass,
banging against the suitlegs
to see what was inside.
Still the mothers gazed, skin
under their eyes like gray
pouched hills with houses
barely visible miles off.
Sun moved in their hair
as my fingers, so lightly,
had stroked your arm, still
in its gold girlish coils.
After all the years of waiting,
to have understood so little
about what we love, now to see
what you, my mother, know,
the far shine of vapor, grass,
houses where I may never return.

Elegy for Hollis Summers

Christmas Eve, I'm remembering
the poet, bald, wisps
of smoke from a cigarette holder.
I offer my poetry thesis. He says,
'I'm a prissy man.' He laughs.
Later he says, 'Do you really want
to say *beautiful eyes?*' And years
after that, after graduation,
when he corners me in the hall, I
accept what may be his last manuscript
of poems, pages speckled and moled
as his head's skin, veined by years
of coffee, gray ash burns, his
exact excisions in blue pen,
its point fine enough to leave
the malignant original faint
as a heartbeat he wanted to know.
'Mr Summers,' I always called him,
despite his protest, refusing
to say *Hollis*, as he asked, holding
off the decades his body wore
when I first heard in his office
the Southern drawl of ancestors.
And giving his book back, wanting
not to tell him what was obvious
and half said, the pain of loves
lost in the words, I knew I would
hurt him with truth he taught me,
fumbling for what survived cuts
like a man's flesh. He stiffened
as each line bit back into him,
a gentleman I now remember. Joy,
duty, love, something made him
send a new poem each Christmas.
Maybe just manners. That hand precise
to the end as the girlish voice
of my aunts: 'Say the poem, David.'

A nettling way, making me live
alone as I try to worry out loud
what once he braved in words,
beginning with *Sir*. And then, *Hollis*.

Moles in Spring

Home from school my daughter's curled
to hide from pain, the grub
of her body knee-to-cheek enfurled

at the center of her shadowed room.
Something's scuttling in her,
little claws of hurt that bloom

into bloodflow. Or worse, a blunt
passerby she cannot welcome,
like the mole she ferried for us

years back, its dog-licked hide
her knot of pain, her care,
and she so comely and fair, the kind

to dazzle a wild thing with a look.
For her yellow hair slipped
like a gown at temple, hooked

in those flashed, flying eyes, I
myself have melted to grass
where cardinals pranced, the sly

watch they kept no barrier at all.
They'd play, too, as we did,
leaping. Around the sun we rolled

until limply we fell and listened.
There under the edge went
tunnels like veins, dark's whim,

a mysterious miner, one I said
I heard, almost, and she,
clever as ever put down her head

in dirt's hold, blinked, lay open
all the looks she had, held
deep in that innocence, and, *Oh,*

yes, cried she, *he's back, Daddy!*
He didn't die or leave me!
Undead, where is that Spring

I dreamed a harm to handle moles,
keep-safe of all I'd sown?
Now I dream of arms. I want to kill

a beast of claws, snout, and bone,
all stepping darkness near.
Yet how to know which is the one,

I asked the mother of my love? Go,
said she, just watch your fill.
Listen as love does. You'll know.

Electric days come back and dirt is
greenly wet. My girl lies down.
Over lawns come newly owlish cries

of boys just past our boundary lines.
I wish they would go home.
I wish the mole would gag and die.

Lyons' Den

What happened to those years, what matchpack
or key with no lock lies
in your desk drawer to be touched again?

In this bar, anonymous as night, a young man
waiting tables wants to be someone.
Hasn't he had to wait all your life?

Tell the truth, merely weeks.
Dark, though, and dark men, some scarred,
who grope at her tits and ass, the waitress,

who she is unimportant now. Five thirty,
shops closed, no rush yet, she gazes
at the blue ocean's breast. You want to ask

what she sees. Tell the truth: you want
what's under her fishnet stockings,
what coos for the legless guitarist whose wheeled

begging board shuttles the boardwalk each dusk,
who lays where she lays. So what?
Didn't she, closing last night, trail fingertip

down your neck, smile, flash out
her desire, and swear at the stairtop
where you live she'll be squirming? No, only

memory's tangle, dead checks, desk debris,
screws that fit what? Remember how she called
you that name, *Sweet Boy*? Sweat bad

as a dockworker, that blunt shouldering by
of the future, already faded, rouge
thick, dark as blood for those with cash. But

she's nowhere, snow falls on her sidewalks
soft as dust in a guitar hole. You
asked when will she love me? Clenched match-stem

in your teeth as they did, breathed her
flared passage through neon
and beer-rut until she vanished, untouched.

What if you could find her, some guzzle-hole,
howling hello? Years like bats dip
into sight, shake you back to that boy, but go

before you can grab what you wanted. She's just
wing-flutter, history's hissing,
her breath rank as dusk's dumpster

where you'll stand in her alley, tight as a lock,
key lost, until she comes. So wait, fear
nothing. Or else you may remember it all again.

Fieldswirl, October

Fog so thick the cows beyond the fence slide
    in and out of focus as I follow
my dogs, the morning's metasticizing ooze
    eating first light, then meat,

yet still faint dragons loom through dewlens
    dropped by flying spiders, each
humped, irridescent spine spewing the steam
    nightdreams dragged to bed, stars

hurled off-orbit like a cat struck by a car. It's
    cattywampus, grandmother said, who
stood in the leafthick to thump it still, and I
    all afternoon in boiling sun sat,

sure I knew I was in hell's hold. Then I saw
    the bull pass in pines, moonlord
of life who kept the fields whole, and I slept
    distant as God from my only home,

unable to answer for the guttings, lies, slicks
    of tears crows racketed around me.
A bare world woke me. Winter, naked crabapple.
    Voices. Movement. Dawn's wiry walk.

A Patch of Weeds

I never learned the names of plants, trees
not easy either, unless some event intervened.
The sycamore one friend nestled into, his car
hurtling like the hawk we used to say he was,
austere, tough, who knew everything in books.
Or an oak chapped by lightning no one saw,
standing always there until my neighbor's boy
crumpled with it. He couldn't scream its name.
And where Route 17 veers from a grove of pines,
where fields seemed burned bald by plowmen,
a lulling sun floats, doves swoop for limbs
long gone, the Nansemond River's blue climbs up.
Some wild purple things here. You have to walk,
bend down beside the gravel and glass shards,
the flattened beer cans, ignoring the flashed
fenders of traffic heaving on. Cup one's head.
When I do this, I am with my father dying.
Whatever its name is, I know when I see it
the sleepy faces of my daughters drift to me.

Graduation

Now the hard white glare
comes flat and lies on everything.
Your black dress smoothed and elegant
on the bed, stockings hung over the chintz chair,
your tasteful shoes set shoulder to shoulder,
are habits as perfect as your pearls,

in turn seamless as our weather,
day after day stringing us through
the ordinary this house has learned to keep.
Nothing's out of place, disturbed, or late anymore.
Cool evenings mean our quiet, long study.
Now the last child goes. His room's

heaped shorts and remains
of shirts, wet towels, lovenotes, chemistry
assignments, the kneeless jeans gagging still
his doorway, his clipped-from-magazine
nudes fluttering on the wall –
tomorrow they'll all be gone,

the broken bed made,
drawers vacant, the floor shining
through a scum of dust like the day we came.
I put on the tuxedo shirt so white and stiff
I feel myself bloom against the silk
slip you're gloved inside.

'Alright, but hurry, hon','
you say, surprised, efficient. So
we lay down again. I say 'We'll see him get his
paper soon, a man like I was not long ago.'
Next I button up, as you have,
remembering the sheets

we spiced and fouled
with youth, sleeping in the scar
of daylight that would leave us swelled against
each other like two wadded fists of print,
edge to edge. 'Hurry,' you hiss,
and grab your shoes and bolt.

A Day Off

There are days when it is hard not to imagine
the unseen, the others always with us,
a day like the color of a shed,
a few feet shuffling on clay,
perfume's old desire
cast under leafless oaks.

In the encircling light of the horizon's flare
you ring her phone endlessly, love's
headache thumps your skull.
The traffic's crazy,
everybody manic. You too.
It's Friday when you park and wait.

Across the street laborers have readied the hole.
Cheap outdoor carpet, froths of petals,
the box hovering under a tent.
Retreated to long, slow draws
on cigarettes, they gaze
when good legs arrive, nothing new.

Near dark you feel their forearms dig fast, soft
curses, comradely words floating away.
Like you, their heads are elsewhere.
They want greasy cabbage, beer,
the chintz chair that smells
of the body. A day off.

In blackness these hidden angels sing, laughing,
how little life gives them, belly aches,
years piled like dogshit. Butts flare.
They bitch, dropping the box.
They remember women and their love.
With huge hungers they woo the night. It's easy.

Night Pleasures
(Poquoson, Virginia)

Where I come from land lies flat as paper.
    Pine, spruce, holly like dark words
left from a woods. Creeks coil, curve,
    enigmatic as women. To know the depths
you must dream. In the mountains
    for college I walked up and could see
barns, cows, housesmoke, but no boats.
    Hillsides of winesaps, still, perfect.

Here my little boat takes the night Bay.
    One far neon light tosses, a city
people walk alone, its rhythmic
    landscape cut from marshes and cries.
On black water it is all mine, first
    beginnings, endings, love's beauties.
So when I move, it moves under me, and knows me.

Index of titles and first lines

(Titles are in italics, first lines in roman type.)

AUTHORS PUBLISHED BY
BLOODAXE BOOKS

FLEUR ADCOCK
GÖSTA ÅGREN
ANNA AKHMATOVA
SIMON ARMITAGE
NEIL ASTLEY
ATTILA THE STOCKBROKER
ANNEMARIE AUSTIN
SHIRLEY BAKER
GEREME BARMÉ
MARTIN BELL
CONNIE BENSLEY
STEPHEN BERG
ATTILIO BERTOLUCCI
YVES BONNEFOY
MARTIN BOOTH
KAMAU BRATHWAITE
GORDON BROWN
BASIL BUNTING
CIARAN CARSON
ANGELA CARTER
JOHN CASSIDY
JAROSLAV CEJKA
MICHAL CERNÍK
AIMÉ CÉSAIRE
SID CHAPLIN
RENÉ CHAR
GEORGE CHARLTON
EILÉAN NÍ CHUILLEANÁIN
KILLARNEY CLARY
BRENDAN CLEARY
JACK CLEMO
HARRY CLIFTON
JACK COMMON
STEWART CONN
NOEL CONNOR
DAVID CONSTANTINE
CHARLOTTE CORY
JENI COUZYN
HART CRANE
ADAM CZERNIAWSKI
PETER DIDSBURY
STEPHEN DOBYNS
MAURA DOOLEY
KATIE DONOVAN
JOHN DREW
IAN DUHIG
HELEN DUNMORE
DOUGLAS DUNN
STEPHEN DUNSTAN
JACQUES DUPIN
G.F. DUTTON
LAURIS EDMOND
ALISTAIR ELLIOT
STEVE ELLIS
ODYSSEUS ELYTIS
EURIPIDES

DAVID FERRY
EVA FIGES
SYLVA FISCHEROVÁ
TONY FLYNN
VICTORIA FORDE
TUA FORSSTRÖM
JIMMY FORSYTH
LINDA FRANCE
ELIZABETH GARRETT
ARTHUR GIBSON
PAMELA GILLILAN
ANDREW GREIG
JOHN GREENING
PHILIP GROSS
JOSEF HANZLÍK
TONY HARRISON
ANNE HÉBERT
HAROLD HESLOP
DOROTHY HEWETT
SELIMA HILL
FRIEDRICH HÖLDERLIN
MIROSLAV HOLUB
FRANCES HOROVITZ
DOUGLAS HOUSTON
JOHN HUGHES
PAUL HYLAND
KATHLEEN JAMIE
VLADIMÍR JANOVIC
B.S. JOHNSON
LINTON KWESI JOHNSON
JOOLZ
JENNY JOSEPH
SYLVIA KANTARIS
JACKIE KAY
BRENDAN KENNELLY
SIRKKA-LIISA KONTTINEN
JEAN HANFF KORELITZ
DENISE LEVERTOV
HERBERT LOMAS
MARION LOMAX
EDNA LONGLEY
FEDERICO GARCÍA LORCA
GEORGE MacBETH
PETER McDONALD
DAVID McDUFF
MEDBH McGUCKIAN
MAIRI MacINNES
CHRISTINE McNEILL
OSIP MANDELSTAM
GERALD MANGAN
E.A. MARKHAM
WILLIAM MARTIN
JILL MAUGHAN
GLYN MAXWELL
HENRI MICHAUX
JOHN MINFORD

ADRIAN MITCHELL
JOHN MONTAGUE
EUGENIO MONTALE
DAVID MORLEY
RICHARD MURPHY
SEAN O'BRIEN
JULIE O'CALLAGHAN
JOHN OLDHAM
MICHEAL O'SIADHAIL
TOM PAULIN
GYÖRGY PETRI
TOM PICKARD
JILL PIRRIE
SIMON RAE
DEBORAH RANDALL
IRINA RATUSHINSKAYA
MARIA RAZUMOVSKY
JEREMY REED
PETER REDGROVE
ANNE ROUSE
CAROL RUMENS
LAWRENCE SAIL
EVA SALZMAN
SAPPHO
WILLIAM SCAMMELL
DAVID SCOTT
JO SHAPCOTT
SIR ROY SHAW
JAMES SIMMONS
MATT SIMPSON
LEMN SISSAY
DAVE SMITH
KEN SMITH
SEAN MAYNE-SMITH
STEPHEN SMITH
EDITH SÖDERGRAN
PIOTR SOMMER
MARIN SORESCU
LEOPOLD STAFF
PAULINE STAINER
EIRA STENBERG
MARTIN STOKES
KAREL SYS
RABINDRANATH TAGORE
JEAN TARDIEU
D.M. THOMAS
R.S. THOMAS
TOMAS TRANSTRÖMER
MARINA TSVETAYEVA
FRED VOSS
ALAN WEARNE
NIGEL WELLS
C.K. WILLIAMS
JOHN HARTLEY WILLIAMS
JAMES WRIGHT
BENJAMIN ZEPHANIAH

For a complete catalogue of books published by Bloodaxe, pleaee write to:
Bloodaxe Books Ltd, P.O. Box 1SN, Newcastle upon Tyne NE99 1SN.